Why Are We Here?

A Meditation on Canada

Why
Are We
Here?

A Meditation on Canada

Mary Jo Leddy

NOVALIS

© 2019 Novalis Publishing Inc.
Cover design: Martin Gould
Cover painting: Naol Amensisa Ketema, age 8, from Ethiopia
Photo of painting: Alex Usquiano
Layout: Audrey Wells

Published by Novalis

Publishing Office
1 Eglinton Avenue East, Suite 800
Toronto, Ontario, Canada
M4P 3A1

Head Office
4475 Frontenac Street
Montréal, Québec, Canada
H2H 2S2

www.novalis.ca

Cataloguing in Publication is available from Library and Archives Canada.

ISBN: 978-2-89688-580-0

Printed in Canada.

We acknowledge the support of the Government of Canada.

5 4 3 2 1   23   22   21   20   19

In memory of Chris Lind
In gratitude for Michael Creal
and for Beverly Keeshig-Soonias
as we have grown up together

About the Cover

The painting featured on the cover is an impression of the area around Manitoulin Island in Ontario. The artist is Naol Amensisa Ketema, an 8-year-old boy from Ethiopia; he painted it during the Romero House summer camp. This was Naol's first encounter with the landscape of the North. There is the blue and green of the forest and lake and the vibrant colours of the plants. In the middle is a drawing of a group of people gathered around a fire. They could be sitting on a flower or on the back of a turtle.

Contents

I

Beginning Here

⟨≁⟩

A story is told of the encounter between a Tsimshian chief and one of the first European explorers as he arrived on the Pacific northwest coast, in the area now known as British Columbia.

"*Why are you here?*" asked the chief.

We have no report of what the explorer answered. We do know the question is with us still – if we are still, if we pay attention. The question winds its way through the centuries and up through the layers of soil and self and spirit.

The question about the meaning and purpose of life is as ancient as it is always new. It is deeply personal and worthy of lifelong, longer than life, consideration.

It is also a question that shapes cultures, nations and empires. Much depends on whether we have the courage to hear this question and allow it to search out our future as a country. I am convinced that the question of the Tsimshian chief now addresses us as a country. For we are all here and we are all now, Indigenous peoples, settlers and newcomers. This remains and must become even more our question together: Why are we here at this time and in this place called Canada?

The question of the Tsimshian chief is stunning in its simplicity. It must be taken to heart and kept in mind and lived beside in a daily way. It invites us to a more meditative way. It involves dwelling below and beyond the surfaces of lesser questions and answers. Thus, the following reflections include, but are not limited by, the insights of artists, political and economic analyses and historical research. My indebtedness to many thinkers and writers will be more evident in the endnotes of this book.

However, the following reflections are ultimately spiritual considerations, religious perspectives in and for a post-secular age. I am convinced that, if we listen to the question of the Tsimshian chief in all its length and breadth and depth, it resounds as a fundamental spiritual question, one that lies beneath the surface of our more obvious preoccupations and conventional ways of seeing as individuals and as a country. I have a hunch about the significance of this question. However, I do not have certainty. Each reader will have to engage this question personally and to discern what is solid and sure in the following reflections.

Although I have drawn on some ancient wisdom in attending to the question of the Tsimshian chief, I have also discovered fresh insights from the perspectives of newcomers to this country: not only from the newest generation of children but also from immigrants and refugees. I have lived with these newcomers and have listened to them. Who you listen to affects what you hear. Where you live determines what you see. Things change when you hear the echoes of the past together with the voices of the future. It is clarifying to see the place where you have always lived with a fresh set of eyes. This is the context of our faith and doubts, the crucible of our imagination and hopes.

Stories from a Northern Lake and a Southern City

A Splendid Space

For the last 26 years I have lived with refugees, many of them children. They have become the eyes of my eyes and the ears of my ears. Through their eyes I have seen a country that is better than I thought and worse than I knew. Through their ears I have heard the clear bell of the question from the Tsimshian chief. *Why are we here?*

Let me tell you two stories that served to introduce me not so much to answers but to insights into this question. One story takes place on a northern lake and the other on a little street in downtown Toronto.

In the summer, the refugees I live with discover that the direction of hope lies north. This is the time when we, a group of about 50 refugees and their Canadian friends, go for a week-long vacation among the lakes and forests near Manitoulin Island. This is the place which is also known by Indigenous peoples who live there as Turtle Island. However, it is still a new and unknown land to the refugee campers who come from all over the world.

During the months preceding this trip, their first and only experience of Canada has taken place in Toronto, a city where they already feel somewhat at home. They will have studied English and learned something in school about the history, culture and political structure of Canada. This information they have memorized dutifully, carefully.

However, the burden of this obligatory history begins to lighten as we drive north on Highway 400 in a yellow school bus and a caravan of cars, past the suburbs and smaller towns and beyond cottage country until we reach the road leading to Manitoulin Island. For the next week these newcomers will "discover" Canada and will begin to understand why they, and we, are here.

I recall the day at camp when a small group of refugees was led out on a hike following a rugged trail overlooking the North Channel of Georgian Bay. After an hour or more of sweaty hiking over the La Cloche mountain range of white granite and majestic pines, one of the older men, from eastern Europe, climbed up to the top of the promontory, looked out over the far-reaching landscape, raised his hands to the sky and shouted, "Canada, I love you!" In that moment, he took this country to heart.

Later that afternoon, after arriving at their lunch destination on the edge of crystal-clear Horseshoe Lake, some of the kids from the Horn of Africa made their discovery – and their own promises. They were shown a large cliff leaning out over this cool, spring-fed lake. They raced up the slope to the rock edge, glistening, screaming with glee. Then they jumped off, toes pointing down and wings outspread, turning towards the land as they flew, saluting with their right arm to some unseen flag, to this their country, to this their place. That was the day they became Canadians.

For the past 26 summers, I have pondered this experience they had of the northern wilderness and why it instantly became so important to these young newcomers, most of whom had lived in large urban centres in other countries, many of whom would eventually choose to settle in more populated areas in the south.

In the mind of my heart this insight has slowly taken shape. I recalled that anthropologists have suggested that identity usually takes shape along two vectors: the sense of time and the sense of space. If one of those vectors of identity is weaker, the other becomes stronger in the balancing act of identity. For better or worse, our sense of the timeline history of "modern" Canada is relatively young and even weak. Four hundred years is neither very long nor epic as the history of nations goes. The history of the Indigenous peoples in this place is longer and more complex by thousands of years. However, many of those histories have been diminished or destroyed, and only now are in the process of being slowly recovered and reclaimed.

In the Canada of the early European settlers and even today, history is a somewhat thin and fragile line of identity.

It is not surprising, then, that a sense of geography and space would and still does become so pivotal for newcomers to this country. In the boreal space of northern Ontario, my refugee neighbours felt that they could belong here, that they could live here and grow here, that they could care for this place. It was not their "native land," to be sure, but it had become a "promised land." They knew it was the homeland of the First Nations, they knew that people from many nations had settled here before them – and they felt welcome. They noticed that there were no immigration officers at the entrance to Manitoulin Island asking them to justify their existence. They were no longer in question and Canada was no longer a question to be answered on an exam. They had arrived not to conquer and own the land, but to live in it. The newcomers caught a glimpse of themselves as inhabitants of this place.

As the kids flew into the water, I saw them shimmer with gratitude in the sunlight. Through the eyes of my eyes I could see that geography was as important as history as a ground for beginning to live here, for belonging. As I watched the kids soar out from the rock and into the sky, I saw my country as though for the first time, in all its spacious splendour. It was a moment when we were, each of us, upheld by wonder, when we all felt grounded, gathered in and free. It was a moment of original gratitude.

These have been moments of grace in my summer meditations: precious times when I have taken a second look at the country called Canada. The people from elsewhere – and from here – have taught me how to say thank you in many different languages: *Gracias, Shukran, Miigwech* … thank you to the trees, to the waters, to the animals, to the First Peoples, to the early settlers, to my ancestors who came on coffin ships from Ireland to survive, to all that is living, growing and giving and here.

A Place for the Common Good

I will also tell a story that provides another and important urban perspective on this northern point of reference. It unfolded over the last 26 years, as I have lived with refugees in an old three-storey brick house in a middle-class area in the west end of Toronto. In this neighbourhood we have struggled every day, in small but real ways, with the very big question that we struggle with as a city and as a country: *What do we hold in common?*

The answer was not obvious and it was a long time coming. As neighbours we did not have an automatic set of common values, shared interests, a common language or religion. We came from diverse cultures and had different political views and educational backgrounds. In this mixed-income area, it seemed as if we just existed side by side, hoping for the best and sometimes fearing the worst.

When we first moved onto this little side street, I was completely oblivious to the neighbours on the street. However, *they* certainly did notice us and all the "different" people who moved in and out of the Romero House building. That difference soon exploded the apparently bland indifference of the neighbours. When we made an application to renovate our old coach house garage in the backyard, many of the neighbours organized and went down to City Hall to put a stop to our plans. Even though this had been a "no-name neighbourhood," a motley group had quickly united in their fear of the strange and unknown people who seemed to pose a serious threat. Much was said that many would later regret: the proposed renovations would create a den of thieves, a place for drug dealers and prostitutes and peeping Toms. For a while I was sure we would have to move out of the neighbourhood. I wondered what we could possibly hold in common. In the absence of any positive sense of being together, a neighbourhood had taken shape through a negative sense of who and what they were against.

However, slowly, very slowly, over many years and through a thousand acts of kindness, we became neighbours. We learned how to respect differences in a way that went beyond indifference. In time, we gathered together in local meetings to decide on a name for this particular area of the city.

The neighbourhood really began to take shape with the decision to hold a street party. It was intended to be a small gathering, but it quickly became larger and was open to anyone who wanted to contribute to the potluck supper or the talent show. Now, more than 20 years later, this street party is considered one of the most significant community events in the neighbourhood and in the city. To celebrate the 25th anniversary of Romero House, the neighbours chipped in to cover the costs of a group of Anishinaabe dancers who opened the street party. All of us, the settled and the newcomers, were welcomed to the traditional land of the Haudenosaunee, Huron Wendat, Anishinaabeg and Mississauga of the New Credit.

Over the years, one could say that we have all walked through walls. There is now room enough for anyone who wants to contribute to the neighbourhood – by tending community gardens, planning the small parkettes, doing an inventory of trees in the area, attending meetings to give feedback on proposals for new developments, analyzing the traffic flows along the local streets, and preparing data on the schools and social services that would be needed for an expected increase in children in the area. We have found a positive ground for being together. There remain problems to be solved, small conflicts to be settled. But we now know we share something in common.

It was during one of the first street parties that I realized that we, as neighbours, did hold something in common. What we held in common was the street itself – another insight that was stunning in its simplicity.

Over time, this simple insight began to alter my imagination of the place I lived in and shifted some of the conceptual structures in my mind. I needed time to think through the thicket of my new thoughts. I began to see that each of the houses on the street occupied space that is usually described as "private property," the space of the personal, the family and the home. We learned that being a good neighbour does not necessarily mean going in and out of each other's houses, as family and friends do. What good neighbours share is another kind of space, the in-between space which is particularly evident in the concrete reality of the street. *This is the space that none of us owns but all of us are responsible for*. It is the space where the children play, the space that good neighbours keep clean and beautiful and safe. The street also signifies many other realities that none of us own but all of us are responsible for: the quality of air and water, the safety of the streets, the health of the trees and parks, the accessibility of swimming pools and libraries, the viability of small local businesses.

This is the kind of place and space that all can belong to, can contribute to, can share in common. The differences remain, the houses and businesses remain private property, but there is also the space in between that is the place of neighbourliness. Neither personal nor political, this is the common space, the place of the commons. That space is lost when anyone or any group tries to control or dominate it, to claim it as a right or to treat it as private property. It can also be lost when no one takes responsibility for it.

This small street, as I will suggest in the following reflections, is a significant example of what it might mean to build a good country: not a great country, but a good country – one with a sense of the common good.

This will involve considering our particular place in the world. And doing so slowly, thoughtfully, carefully – in a meditative sort of way.

Considering Our Place in the World

The reflections that follow do not automatically suggest a certain public policy or support a particular political party. They do not justify or critique a particular economic or political theory. I am simply suggesting some foundational considerations that may help us take the question of the Tsimshian chief to heart.

One thing is sure: we ignore his question at our peril. But if we hear it out in all its length and depth and thickness, we may hear within us the beginning of a deeper YES to being here in this time and place. This would mean, for starters, saying at least this: We are not here just to make a living. We are not here just to go shopping. We are not here just to look out for ourselves – and our own barbeques. We are meant for more than this. And then we may discover a real NO has slowly replaced the grumbling and whining and grinding. NO to taking it all for granted. NO to saying never and not here and not now.

And YES to attentiveness to one another, to the kids playing in the street, to those neighbours who need help with their huge garbage bins or with their snow shovelling. And YES to talking in the street. And YES to taking the time for this.

Taking the question of the chief to the mind of our hearts would mean taking ourselves seriously. It would mean considering that we are here for a reason, that we are more than tourists passing through this country on the way to someplace else.

It would also mean taking the Indigenous peoples (First Nations, Inuit and Métis) seriously and gratefully. They walked these streets in the west end of Toronto while they were still pathways to the lake. They are buried here.

I believe we are at the beginnings of a new day, in a new moment, in the relationships between Indigenous peoples and settlers. This is a foundational moment for the country called Canada, a moment of refounding that is as full of peril as it is of promise.

Thinking about one's own country is long, hard work. It takes time: a lifetime … longer than a lifetime. It involves listening to many and various groups of people. It implies taking one's bearings from the place or places that you have an affection for. Nevertheless, this is good work because the question of the Tsimshian chief is worthy of great attention. We are so often trapped in the maze of how to manage our economic and social life that we lose our way: How will we develop our resources? How will we deal with America? We need to think about WHY we are here in this time and place before we consider HOW to proceed further. Many of our efforts, to determine what and how we should do things, shake down and simplify as the meaning and purpose of it all becomes clearer.

As we consider our own lives, there are some moments when we wonder about the significance and purpose of our existence. *Why am I here?* How we consider this question affects what we do with our lives, how we will spend our time and with whom. Our answer to this question will determine why we get up in the morning, if we enjoy our work and whether we can sleep easy at night.

Why are we here? It is a question that organizations and institutions and countries ponder from time to time: there are efforts to clarify goals, mission statements, even constitutions and treaties.

Why are we here? It is at once a liberating and terrifying question. It takes us forward but also behind and below – and through. It opens a prior question that surfaced on that rock cliff over the pure spring water of a northern lake and in the middle of a little neighbourhood street.

And that question is:

Where is here?

2

Where Is Here?

←↔→

I t is not often that we hear the question of the Tsimshian chief asked so clearly and so simply. We seem to be a very large country with a relatively small sense of purpose. All too often we leave it to politicians and professors to debate the topic of Canadian identity, to articulate Canadian values, to assess the various histories of Canada. We are not lacking in individual courage and talent and creativity, but we have a rather modest sense of our place in the world. We can be counted on to cheer for our team at the Olympics and we take pride in the individual achievements of Canadians: the singers, the athletes, the scientists, the successful and the saints. However, a particular sense of national purpose often seems beyond us. The "Peace, Order and Good Government" embedded in the British North America Act of 1867 articulates a modest goal, although at times it seems magnificent considering the world we live in.

There are moments when we catch a glimpse of why we are here: watching Gord Downie sing the anthems of a generation during his last tour of the country and the long, sad song of the journey home of 12-year-old Chanie Wenjack; mourning the loss of the young hockey players in Humboldt, Saskatchewan, as if they belonged to all of us; singing "Hallelujah" with Leonard Cohen as his body was taken up the Côte-des-Neiges hillside in Montreal; celebrating the great generosity of the small town of Gander, Newfoundland, as they welcomed those who had "come from away."

Nevertheless … we hesitate. Not always, but more than is necessary.

As I have pondered our moral and political hesitancies as a country, I have become more aware of how our thoughtless regard for the significance of being HERE has much to do with the economic and political systems within which we live and move and have our being: we are constrained by a long history of colonialism in which we have been both victims and perpetrators, and we are captivated by the dynamic of late capitalism that fuels a consumer culture.

The Constraints of Colonialism

Canada is a colony. This is a hard fact that many are reluctant to admit. Once upon a time, Canada may have been a colony, we think, but not here, not now. Canada is now a relatively rich nation, a somewhat significant country, or so we think. We do not hear the chains of history rattle as we run our own elections and have our own flag. In the 21st century, it seems strange to think of Canada as a colony. It is a strange but necessary reckoning.

The political and economic realities of Canada are now embedded as a colonial mindset within this country. It is that mindset that holds us in captivity. Hesitant.

A cursory look at the history of this place, since the time of the first European settlers, indicates that we have always been the colony of some imperial power. We have been a colony of the French empire, the centre of the fur trade and the mission territory of the Catholic church. We have been a colony of the British empire, a vast warehouse of natural resources, supplying the empire through a network of banking and transportation. And since the end of the Second World War, Canada has become a colony of the American empire. Our particular status of sharing a continent with the greatest world power is not always obvious. We seem to be "best friends," "good neighbours" and "allies." We also know THERE (in Washington and New York) is where the head office is and where who really decides what happens HERE can be found.

Others have named us. The French and the British saw this place as harsh and forbidding, but also as a storehouse for resources of great value. Americans have tended to see us as boring, compliant, trustworthy, nice and safe. A colony without significant power. A place with resources that could be counted on. The 2018 free trade negotiations now mark a significant shift in these perceptions – or a confirmation of them.

Our challenge to find our own voice and our own place is one we share with many other countries in the world who are struggling to move beyond the habits of mind and heart that have been shaped by imperial powers. We live in a world profoundly shaped by the aspirations of peoples who are struggling to free themselves from a history of being dominated by imperial powers. Countries such as India, Mexico and Nigeria are at least fortunate in this: they know they have been oppressed by an imperial power and that this has afflicted them in their hearts and minds, in their souls and bodies. The post-colonial period begins to dawn in consciousness when people begin to say, "We exist. We are here."

Canadians, in general, have been much less aware of how the experience of colonialism has restricted their sense of who they are and what they can become.

Nevertheless, the subtle constraints of colonialism affect our ability to think about HERE, about where we are and what we are about. A colonial person tends to focus on the realities of empire, on the place and people elsewhere who determine and influence what goes on here. For colonial peoples, the centres of power and influence are always someplace else. To read the histories of the first settlers in this place is to learn a great deal about what was happening in Europe, especially in Paris and London. In the 20th century we were (and still are) more attuned to what was (and still is) happening in New York and Washington than in Ottawa or in the stock exchanges of Montreal and Toronto. As our cosmopolitan prime minister Pierre Elliott Trudeau wisely observed almost 40 years ago, living next to the United States is like sleeping next to an elephant. You are aware of its every move.

The reality of living in a colony is that the centres of education, the significant ideas and the latest in art and fashion are almost always created someplace else, not here. The decisions affecting business and politics are usually made elsewhere in the economic imperial centres of finance and power. What is interesting and worth thinking about, worth critiquing, is often in another place, not here. Living on the periphery of power creates its own particular sense of powerlessness. It makes it difficult for us to imagine that it is we ourselves who can and must answer the question of the Tsimshian chief. We cannot weigh in on the question until we feel our own weight and significance and know that our answer is of some consequence. We need to remove our colonial blinders so we can see the very real goodness and the real evil that exists HERE among us and within us. We need to see the ways in which we are both the victims and the perpetrators of colonialism.

The constraints of colonialism and the captivity of consumerism make it difficult for us to see, as I have suggested, that Canada is better than we know and worse than we think.

Yet, we cling to our myth of innocence, that we are good people who are incapable of doing really bad things. It is one of the temptations of a colonial people who tend to think that bad things are done *to* them rather than *by* them. The power to do great good and evil lies elsewhere, not here, not in a relatively powerless colony. It makes it harder for us to see the colonies that exist within our colony, the ghettos of poverty and the gated communities of the rich, the places of privilege and the forgotten regions and reserves of this country.

We have developed what I would call a branch plant morality that puts the blame for wrongs at the head office, which is almost always elsewhere, anywhere but here. It is a dangerous innocence and blinds us to the very real good that we are capable of and the evil that we can manage on our own. For example, many Canadians protested mightily against the conduct of the US government during the Vietnam war, but didn't notice that Agent Orange was being produced by Uniroyal Ltd. in the lovely little town of Elmira, Ontario. This toxic chemical defoliated the jungles of Vietnam, killing thousands of people. It continued to poison people living in the farmlands of Ontario for many years after. Our myth of innocence blinds us not only to the evil we are capable of but also to the very real goodness that exists within the heart of America itself. It was Americans who marched in protest and objected to the use of Agent Orange on the vegetation and the human beings of Vietnam.

In more recent years, we have turned over recent Canadian citizens to be imprisoned and tortured in other places. The cases of Maher Arar and Hassan Diab are but two examples of the way that racism affects our response to injustice. The fact that they were "Middle Eastern" seemed to trump the fact that they are Canadian citizens.

On June 23, 1985, Air India flight 182, travelling from Canada to Europe, exploded over the Atlantic Ocean near the coast of Ireland. Three hundred and twenty-nine people were murdered: 268 were Canadian citizens, and 126 were children. "It was the single worst act of terrorism in Canadian history." Yet for almost 20 years this was considered an Indian tragedy rather than a Canadian tragedy. These people were excluded from our universe of moral concern.

Our colonial resentments against the head offices elsewhere fuel our tendencies to define ourselves in terms of who and what we are against. Being Canadian means being anti-American. Being Canadian means being against Toronto. I think these considerations situate the long and seemingly fruitless conversation about Canadian identity, a conversation that really should be about whether we hold anything in common as a country. Is our national purpose simply to survive? To be secure and prosperous? Is that all? If this is our only purpose, we will inevitably become a nation of groups held together by a series of real or invented threats. A nation that is unsure of its positive purpose will resort to symbols as a kind of glue to hold the country together. It will roll out the flag and parade the Mounted Police, and cheer for the national hockey team at international events.

The Perpetual Dissatisfaction of a Consumer Culture

It is also difficult to stop and consider HERE when we are so very busy getting by or getting ahead. For many in this consumer culture, life is a driven experience. We produce, and produce to consume, more things, more experiences, and so we are consumed in the process. Those who cannot produce, such as the unemployed, the aged, and people with disabilities, are consumed by guilt and despair and depression. Consumerism is the defining shape of corporate capitalism, and it afflicts almost everyone throughout the world. Jeans, Coke, music are the trademarks in the streets of the global reach of consumerism. The pervasive and subtle imperialism of this global culture is difficult to resist because it hides its radical materialism beneath the promise of satisfying some of our most human desires. The message of advertising is that you will be happy if you get more and more; you will get an identity and be able to buy meaning and purpose for your life. The conviction instilled by consumerism is that happiness lies in getting more and more, bigger and bigger. This craving for more is fuelled by the advertising industry, which seduces us into thinking that what we have and who we are is never enough, that where we are is never as important as where we are going. Consumerism sets up within us a craving, a perpetual dissatisfaction not only with what we have, but also with who we are and where we live.

Lest we think that we are unaffected by this most subtle form of imperialism, it is worth remembering that the average Canadian and American will, by the end of his or her life, have "consumed" at least five solid years of advertising alone. This culture of craving and the inevitable dissatisfaction it fosters has now become global, exerting its power in places as diverse as China, India, Brazil, Indonesia and Kazakhstan. This empire of global capitalism exists everywhere, but the centre seems to be nowhere. The effect on local cultures and national aspirations, however, is devastating. And no one can be found to take responsibility for this.

In Canada, as elsewhere, the ethos of global capitalism affects all aspects of our lives: how we understand ourselves, our identity, how we construct the meaning and purpose of our lives. This consumer culture transforms our relationship to the place where we live: we can tend to think of our place in the world as an item that can be bought or sold; we think of loyalty and affection for a place as something that is obsolete because it is unmarketable. National pride can seem quaint or contrived. We are consumers of property and places rather than citizens and inhabitants of neighbourhoods.

Consumerism is a contemporary form of materialism and treats the "place" in terms of its monetary value: what is it worth? Large groups of people are relocated from places they love in order to make a living so some company can make a profit. All over Canada and the United States and through-out the world, cities and towns are abandoned as others are manufactured overnight. Is it any wonder that so few have the luxury of considering the value of the place where they live, the city they work in, the country they are citizens of? The vast forces of the economy have displaced so many, have left them searching for some form of solidarity and protection with family or the few friends who have survived the many steps of moving. It sets the scene for what has been called "the corrosion of character" and the growth of conservative extremism among those who are seeking stability and coher-ence in the midst of their chronic displacement.

The ground beneath our feet is disappearing. The place where we stand and live seems to vanish as we are on the way to someplace else.

The power of these economic forces moves through and beyond national borders and boundaries. Countries seem powerless to control these forces and struggle to maintain some independence – either by joining with other coun-tries or by negotiating trade deals. It makes the struggle for national identity and purpose more difficult but ever more necessary.

We are indeed in captivity. This culture of consumerism has bypassed our national, regional and local borders so that it is now everywhere. Our local cultures are bought and sold, marketed and overlooked. Local cultures have been separated from their roots and have been sold to the highest bidder. These cultures no longer exist to express the sufferings and longings of a people and a community. They are used to market soft drinks, cars and vacation packages. Local talent is used in the opening act for the main event, still called America. Even Indigenous cultures have become hot commodities as ancient music and symbols are bought and sold in the marketplace.

Why are we here? We are here to shop.

We are here to get more and more.

The culture of consumerism is far more dominating and imperious than any political power. It holds our hearts, minds and souls in captivity. It is a culture that is shaped by the worldview of the American empire – faith in the myth of progress: If you just work hard and think smart, things will get better and better. As the dream of a better world and a better America begins to fade, it has been transformed into very materialistic terms: If you just work hard and think smart, you will get more and more.

Before we can even consider the question of the Tsimshian chief, we must free ourselves from the captivity of the consumer culture. This will not be easy, as this culture is enmeshed in our economic system, in our political and social arrangements, in the sense of the meaning and significance of our lives.

To See Where We Are

It is an immense challenge to see one's own culture, to notice the ground beneath our feet. Like fish in polluted water, we do not notice the cultural waters we swim in. In fact, it is probably easier for us to recognize the features of other cultures than to notice those of our own culture, which is like the air we breathe. It is taken for granted, normal. Otherwise known as reality. The Tsimshian chief knew where he lived.

That we may see... There is so much data about Canada – economic analysis, political and social reports ... and a flood of information with lots of questions and many answers. All of this does not necessarily give us insight into where we are at this particular time and place.

In search of insight, we need guides who can see in the fog. We need to listen to the artists who dwell in the realm of the imagination. Sometimes, it is our artists (our writers, musicians, architects and filmmakers) who see beneath the surface, who divine the question below the questions, who imagine and name what is not yet known.

In addition to the artists who help us see in the dark, we also need to see where we are through the eyes of those who are suffering. It is they who see and feel the shadow side of this place called Canada most clearly, and it is they who hope beyond reason in its great promise. We must recognize the authority of those who suffer in seeing, grasping, judging and responding to such things.

Who are the speakers, the artists, the forgotten thinkers, the lesser lights and, most importantly, the victims in this colony? To consider this place from the perspective of those who have suffered here is to begin to think about how power has been wielded for better or worse, about how there are colonies within this colony, about how our failure to acknowledge how the operation of power within this colony has allowed us to wrap ourselves in innocence while abandoning the struggle for a more creative and constructive exercise of power.

The literary critic Northrop Frye understood that for those who live in a colony and are shaped by this perspective, the question to begin with is "WHERE IS HERE?" More ancient civilizations with a longer sense of history may have the luxury and challenge of pondering more individual questions such as "Who am I?" and "What is the meaning and purpose of my life?" However, those shaped by a colonial mindset must begin by considering where they are before they can think about who they are and why they are here.

This kind of searching question is asked differently in different cultures. Countries with a long and deep history, such as those in Europe that have lived through centuries of struggle and defeat and achievement, have become defined by this history. Against this solidity of history, it is possible that the question of the meaning and purpose of life can and should be posed in more personal terms: Why am I here? This is the kind of question that could be posed by a French existentialist after generations of waste and war, after epochs of splendour and power.

However, in a country as young as Canada, in a country that is still taking shape, in a nation emerging from the shadows of colonialism, the question of the meaning and purpose of life cannot only be individual. Self-definition becomes a futile exercise when we do not know the earth beneath our feet, the air we breathe, the context that shapes our way of being in the world.

This means that the most liberating and significant question for those who have been shaped by a colonial consciousness is "Where is here?" To begin by being HERE, by taking HERE as a crucial point of reference. To begin by listening, to capture the cadence of language, the question below the questions, to begin by reading the history of this place not from the perspective of the empire but from the perspective of here.

To begin to really think about what it means for us to live HERE is to take on the weight and significance of this particular country at this particular time in history. It is to assume the particular blessing and burden of Canada.

There have been many studies and analyses of "Canada." These can be helpful, useful. There are many histories of Canada: some old, some new, many revised versions. These are the stories we tell about ourselves or the stories that one group wants to impose on other groups. These are stories of identity, of how we became what we are today. Nevertheless, these histories do not automatically provide us with insight into what is the significance and meaning of this particular country at this particular time in history.

Boundaries of Identity

What is Canada today? Is it a collection of people who share a certain history? Is it a collection of chapters of history in search of a book? Is it those who were here first? Is it a dream? Is it a mindset? Is it a set of particular values? Is it a geography with boundaries? Is it a culture described as "Canadian culture"?

The desire to construct something called "Canadian culture" is particularly tempting given the bland documents that have set out the goals of this country. Much could be said about the word "culture" to describe the underlying coherence of a people in a particular time and place. I am not using this term to refer to a more traditional and somewhat elitist sense of "being cultured" or "being civilized." Rather, I am referring to culture in the more contemporary anthropological sense: the values, the symbols, the codes of communication, the spirit that is expressed through architecture, music, art, political arrangements, sexual and familial and tribal arrangements.

However, I doubt that there is such a thing as "Canadian" culture. Northrop Frye argued this point long ago. He said so out of a profound respect for the way in which the imagination is always located in a particular time and place. "There is something vegetable about the imagination," he wrote. By this he meant that the imagination is rooted in and grows from a very specific experience of people in a place. Once culture is abstracted from that experience of place, it becomes empty, a commodity to be bought and sold.

Frye held that all culture is local, while economics is more properly national and global. We are now in a period in which global economics is moving through and beyond national borders. Global economics and global technology are also destroying local cultures and treating them as a commodity.

Thus, we have a Maritime culture with its particular cadence of music, and its experience of the vast danger and bounty of the sea. We have the culture of Quebec, with its fierce devotion to language and culture and the traces of religion; we have the culture of small-town Ontario and the experience of the particular loneliness and sense of community that could be found there; we have the immensity of the prairie flatlands and the "little houses" that struggled to survive there. There is a residual culture of co-operation that this experience generated, even when it sometimes seems less necessary now. There is a mountain culture and the culture of the west coast where new things seem possible.

Many Indigenous groups have fought bravely to retain some of the vestiges of their cultures. The way in which these peoples were so profoundly uprooted meant that they were dislocated, abstracted from the deepest sources of their spirituality. And yet. And yet. They are here. They live here. They have survived – and more.

Many Canadians have the experience of living in not just one but perhaps several places in this country. For them, being Canadian means learning to live in multiple overlapping cultures. Others discover that they have more in common with similar cultures in other regions than they do with their own regional culture. For example, people who live in large metropolitan areas (Vancouver, Toronto, Montreal) have somewhat similar experiences of being located there than they have with smaller towns within their own region.

Living in between cultures is becoming a kind of identity for more and more Canadians. As described so aptly by the poet Anne Michaels,

> … We sleep between Hudson's Bay and the Great
> Lakes, below geese migrating their secret paths under
> the stars. Here, where great rivers of history converge,
> travelling through the night to wake in another lan-
> guage. It is a city where many work in one language
> and fall in love in another.

Such considerations make us realize that it is difficult to think of Canada as a single unified whole. Our attempts to develop a single version of Canadian history, to articulate a single set of Canadian "values" or a single articulation of Canadian identity have been important but not successful. Our desperate efforts to sustain the Royal Canadian Mounted Police as a symbol of national unity is an affront to the victims who have suffered from the injustices committed by the RCMP.

Many continue to think of hockey as part of the culture that shaped Canada. It is an exciting sport in which people learned to be at home in the winter and on the ice and learned what the values of co-operation and competition meant if played by the rules. But now it can seem that hockey has become a business in which players are bought and sold as mercenaries. It becomes more difficult for the players and the fans to feel a sense of loyalty to the team or an affection for the place they are supposed to represent.

The efforts to define Canada by certain cultural icons have also failed for another reason. Most of these attempts have treated culture as something fixed and frozen or as something deep that could and should be discovered. To say that Canada is a British or French culture is a gross oversimplification. Yet, this is what we do: we debate how waves of immigration have affected the "British" or "French" character of the country. In this we replicate the attitude found in most Western countries that see their national identity or culture as under threat from other cultures. Quebec's long struggle to preserve its culture is heroic given the monoculture of North American consumerism.

The culture debates that have gripped Canada and Quebec have sometimes assumed that culture is something fixed, something that can be defined and settled on. However, a more serious reflection on culture would say that it is a dynamic existential reality, constantly developing and changing. For example, there is no such thing as "British culture." It would be more appropriate to say that there is a culture on the Islands to the north and west of Europe that is a historic combination of the Romans, the Vikings, the Normans, the Celts, and so on. It is the dynamic, interactive history of many overlapping cultures that constitute what we unreflectively refer to as "British culture."

This essentialist view of culture treats it as a thing that has the potential to unite Canadians or to unite Quebec in its nationalist aspirations. It also seems to accomplish this

35

by distinguishing Canadian or Quebec culture and identity from other cultures and identities. However, culture is much more dynamic than this. It is always growing, changing and developing. Just as Canadians move and live and set down roots in various parts of the country, so it is always the case that a person who is called a Canadian is a hybrid, a combination of particular cultures. This is a much more existential view of culture, one that takes account of the dynamic and diverse nature of this country.

The question of the Tsimshian chief remains. *Why are you here?* The reflections on the ways in which consumerism and colonialism deflect this question suggest that some response must involve an attentiveness to the question *Where is here?* This is a question as difficult and as simple as that of the Tsimshian chief.

There have been many fine efforts to define this HERE that we now call Canada: there have been attempts to articulate a Canadian history, Canadian values, Canadian culture or multiculturalism, Canadian political dynamics. The newcomers to this country learn all of this, but does it really help them to live HERE? And does it really help the First Peoples of this place to live once again HERE? And does it help those of us who are now somewhere between the first inhabitants of this land and the relative newcomers to this place?

3

The Original Moment

↤↦

T here is, I believe, an original event, an original moment, either very long or very short, that shapes the subsequent history and direction of a political or social group. It is a moment, full of promise and of peril, whose significance becomes clearer as time goes on. This moment may or may not be articulated fully in the foundational documents of a new political reality. It may not even be recognized at the time as the defining moment.

Every society has a founding myth that serves as a key point of reference as that society moves and develops. It arises out of some foundational experience. Thus, we have the founding myths of Rome or of America that articulate the deepest positive sense of purpose within those once small republics. There are also, for example, the creation myths of various Indigenous peoples. These foundational myths set out a horizon of meaning that identifies a socio-political entity. Such myths also contain the seeds of their own destruction which, if unaddressed and unacknowledged, eventually wreak their own havoc. For example, there is a noble statement in the 1776 American Declaration of Independence: "We hold these truths to be self-evident, that all men are created equal, that they are endowed by their Creator with certain inalienable rights, that among these are Life, Liberty and the Pursuit of Happiness." However, the "men" who were created equal did not include the Indigenous peoples, slaves, and women and children. Each of these groups would suffer in turn from the violence of exclusion, and each of these groups would eventually demand the freedom and dignity they had been denied.

The original moment thus combines light and shadow, sin and grace, just as every culture both reveals and conceals, has strengths and weaknesses. Those who live within a certain culture are often the last ones to see this most clearly. There are those who will proudly see their culture as "the best" or the "greatest," overlooking its fatal weaknesses. Meanwhile, others in the same culture will be painfully aware of the problematic reality of that culture without noticing its hidden strengths and potentialities. It is a challenge to name the particular mix of blessings and burdens in the reality of one's own time and place. Far too many people imagine they are living in another place, not here, or in another time, not now.

All too often the founding myth and genius of the country constituted by Confederation was taken to be the historic compromise between two languages (French and English), cultures (British and French) and religions (Catholic and Protestant) that laid the basis for the respect for tolerance and diversity and led to the respect for what the British North America Act (1867) called "peace, order and good government."

This description of the founding moment of Canada is now undergoing a radical revision. The newer history of Canada articulates that there were or should have been three founding groups in the origin of Canada: the Indigenous peoples, the French and the English. The failure to acknowledge, include and respect the existence and cultures of the Indigenous peoples constitutes what could be called the original sin, the original flaw that lies at the beginnings of this country.

However, before we can think about what this means here and now, before we can analyze the implications politically, socially and historically, we need to try to imagine the original moment of this country. Yes. It is an act of imagination.

I turn to Northrop Frye and Margaret Atwood as guides to imagining the original moment of the country now called Canada. They are not the latest public pundits, but they have a certain wisdom in naming how the particular geography of what is now called Canada was significant in shaping the relationship between the settler cultures and the Indigenous peoples. Their reflections are helpful in understanding many of our present attitudes, our problems and our potential as a contemporary nation.

Their insights into this original moment lay the groundwork for guiding social and political analysis, histories and cultural studies. They have discovered these insights in the space where horizon and ground meet, where the shape of land and rock and sky becomes a furrow in the brain and the imagination of this place. They have listened to the cadence of language and music; they have considered the habits of the heart and the penchant of mind formed in the original experience of the first European settlers as they encountered this land and its inhabitants.

According to Atwood, "Every country or culture has a single unifying and informing symbol at its core." England has the symbol of the Island; America has the symbol of the Frontier. These are not empty symbols: they are embodied in the art and music, public policy and social arrangements and values of these cultures. The unifying and informing symbol for Canada, writes Atwood, is that of Survival.

The Imperative of Survival

In their reflections on the Canadian context, Frye and Atwood gave great weight to the formative experience of the first European settlers as they encountered the Indigenous peoples and the vast geography of this land. These reflections are not the only way of understanding why we are the way we are, but they are helpful. They also reveal how the settlement of this country by successive waves of people from elsewhere has made our response to the Tsimshian chief both difficult and necessary.

The first Europeans entered the waterways of this land through the St. Lawrence River. As they moved up this river, they must have felt overwhelmed by the sheer immensity of the space that surrounded and engulfed them – so unlike any river they had known in western Europe. As Frye and Atwood interpret and then describe this moment, this vast space seemed menacing and indifferent. This sense of threat did not cease when they landed. The land was vast and threatening and mercilessly cold in winter and filled with blackflies and mosquitoes in summer. The waters, the rocks, the impenetrable forests were filled with danger. "Nature seemed indifferent or hostile," Frye wrote. Some of the greatest dangers seemed to come from a strange people who inhabited this wild geography and were at home there. The first challenge facing the European settlers, French and English, was to survive – not to explore and dominate, but merely to survive. From the beginning, the sense of threat and the imperative of survival blinded them to the summons of a new land, the promise held in the encounters with new peoples, the call to a new way of being.

The imperative of survival in the cold and rugged North, of what would become Canada, moved the first European settlers to build little garrisons in which they could huddle together and protect each other from the forces of nature and the wild people they called "the Indians." "A garrison is a closely knit and beleaguered society, and its moral and social values are unquestionable." Within these garrisons of survival, according to Frye and Atwood, the European settlers developed an ethos of cooperation that would later become embedded in the Constitution and the various institutions of the emerging nation of Canada – respect for peace, order and good government. The struggle to survive was not without its moments of joy: in the settlement of Port Royal, Champlain inaugurated "The Order of Good Cheer," a splendid gathering of the community to sustain its members through the long winters.

The first settlers in Canada learned how to survive in communities in which people lived in the shelter of each other. They weathered storms of various kinds together, including fierce weather, crop failures, hostile encounters with "the Indians," and more. They kept each other safe and sound. This foundational experience can be evoked more easily than it can be defined. Some would say that it is this experience that lies at the core of the public policies that later developed in Canada and formed what is now called the social safety net. Survival through social solidarity became one of the original social policies developed in areas of the country threatened by a combination of economic forces and natural disasters: the co-op movement in the fisheries of the Maritimes and the agriculture and economic cooperatives on the prairies during the Great Depression in the 1930s. It was these foundational experiences that also shaped the imagination behind the innovative social policy that came to be known as Medicare.

There was a period before Confederation in which the early settlers learned how to survive from the First Peoples, who also taught the settlers the art of negotiation and compromise.

In this original moment, the settlers measured their lives against a vast horizon. They learned that survival meant co-operating with each other. This would persist as the positive aspect of the founding experience. There was also a negative dimension in that respect, for a communal ethos was often triggered by a sense of real or perceived threat from some unknown force.

This grace and this sin persist today.

If the Tsimshian chief had met these early settlers and asked them, "Why are you here?" they might have answered,

We are here to explore.

We are here to do business.

We are here to save souls.

Yet, they may also have answered, as they often did after long journeys and bitter suffering: *We are here to survive.*

The Persistence of the Garrison Mentality

The garrison mentality also had its shadow side, a shadow that seems to lengthen even unto today. The garrison as a culture often took shape as people pulled together because there was a common threat. In other words, it was a culture defined more by what/who it was against rather than by what/who it was for. In response to the geography of this land, the first Europeans shaped a culture that was not at home in nature and a society that was seriously alienated from the people who were the original inhabitants of this place. If there is such a thing as an original sin in the history of a nation, this is it.

This foundational experience also has a shadow side that often remains invisible to those who are within it. To see this shadow side, we need another set of eyes. We need the ancient seeing eyes of the Indigenous peoples and we need the fresh eyes of the newcomers. These are the groups who remain outside of the garrisons and who, from this perspective, see the long shadows cast by the efforts within Canada to defend against the threats posed by larger and unknown forces.

Ancient Eyes

The foundational fact that the land now called Canada was and is the home of the Indigenous peoples has resulted in an original injustice that is only now being addressed. The survival of the settlers was often bought at the expense of the survival of the Indigenous peoples. The extent of their loss is something that only they can measure fully. These peoples were treated as a "threat" to the more "civilized society" that lived in the garrisons. They were "wild" and not "like us": yet these locals had lived here for thousands of years.

The Final Report of the Truth and Reconciliation Commission of Canada is an important invitation to measure the real history of this country. We can suggest that the loss is not only to the Indigenous peoples, but also to the settlers who came to this country. Our loss of a genuine, respectful and just relationship with the original peoples has afflicted our relationship to the land and geography of this place.

While there may have been some initial efforts for the settlers to cooperate with and learn from the Indigenous peoples, the country called Canada developed through a long, sad history of successive governments trying to separate the people in the garrison of "civilization" from the "wild strangers." Politicians and religious leaders decided the "Indians" should become like us and learn the ways of the garrison. The settlers were so busy teaching the Indians that they missed the most important lessons the Indians had to teach.

There were those settlers who were self-taught, as it were, those who learned to love the land, the villages and cities. There were *coureurs des bois* (traders) who lived and worked with the First Peoples. There were the teachers who threw away the books, the artists who paid attention to the wind and the water. There were those who left the garrison and learned something about this place.

There was a world of difference between the people who lived within the garrisons and those who live outside them. There was a world of difference between those who learned how to subdue the wilderness and those who treated it with care and respect.

The ancient eyes of the Tsimshian chief help us to see how we have tended to treat the natural world in this place now called Canada.

Managers and Modernizers

We no longer build little garrisons in the snow. In fact, many of the inventions of modern technology have made it easier for us to live in the winter: with snow blowers and skidoos, with insulation and central heating, we have become comfortable in the cold. We have been able to traverse wide expanses of snow by car and railway. We have been able to fly to warmer climates in the midst of winter. The history of the nation-state called Canada unfolded as technology (the railway) made it possible for the settlers to push ever further west, clearing the plains of the Indigenous peoples who were living there. It was a cruel clearing that left the inhabitants of the land decimated.

In short, we are no longer afraid of the land we live in. We have learned to use it, to dominate it, to buy parcels of it and to sell its resources. The tragedy is that the European settlers went from a fear of nature to a much more utilitarian view of nature without learning to care for it. The development of Canada became possible by what Frye called "the conquest of nature by an intelligence that does not love it."

And most of the early settlers never learned to appreciate the Indigenous peoples who had inhabited the land for centuries, who had learned how to live within it. These peoples were invisible, expendable. They were in the way as Canada began to push its way west and north.

As the economist Harold Innis wisely observed, Canada quickly became defined as a colony with a storehouse of natural resources or "staples." After the fur trade there was the turn towards the staples that could act as the engine of the new modern economy: wood, fish, trees, wheat. Bigger and better machines helped us to mine the natural resources of the country, which became the fuel for the economy. Oil. Minerals. Gas. Uranium. One of our most lucrative exports at this time is the expertise we have developed through Canadian mining and oil companies. Inhabitants of the country have used all the developments of modern technology to exploit the natural resources of the area which, after Confederation, came to be known as Canada.

Many of the first American settlers began to think of themselves as masters of their universe. A more hospitable terrain and climate made the westward expansion of the United States more feasible. In the process, the frontier mentality began to shape the American Dream. Americans were Lone Rangers, walking tall and alone. Many of those who went west in search of a dream felt stretched and made bigger by the vastness of the space. The first Canadian settlers, on the other hand, did not so much see themselves as masters of the universe as the managers of this territory.

Canadian commercial companies tamed the wilderness of this place through the use of modern technology and hard manual labour. However, they not only used the machinery of modernity; they were also shaped by it. Utilizing ever more efficient technology, the mercantile companies were able to develop a transportation grid (railways, canals, steamships); to refine the methods of fishing; to expand the harvesting of the farmlands; to mine and refine the metals of the Canadian Shield.

In the process, Canadians made a living by treating nature merely as a resource: an object, a thing that could be used and refined. We treated nature as a possession, something that we owned, that we had a right to.

This attitude and these assumptions blinded these settlers to the fact that these resources had been used for centuries, in simpler form, by the Indigenous peoples. The new managers of these resources began to clear the land of the people who had cared for it and respected it. And the land was cleared, violently, through disease and decrees and false treaties. The presence of the Indigenous peoples decreased and, in some cases, they disappeared.

The settlers became efficient managers of the natural resources in the country, but failed to gain the wisdom of a people who had learned not how to become masters of the wilderness but inhabitants of a place.

There have been historic conflicts and differences between the French and English in Canada, between the people of the nation of Quebec and the rest of Canada, but the geography of northern Quebec is very much like the geography of northern Ontario. To the businessman, the manager of commercial investors from here and elsewhere, the North is a place to be claimed and mined. Here, once again, we are repeating the patterns of the past: treating this place as a resource to be harvested, mined, siphoned off; ignoring the fact that this is a homeland to Indigenous peoples. Places and people can be managed out of existence, today as long ago.

We have lost many of our Indigenous guides through the wilderness. Some of them have lost their way. Some have been pushed out of the way. Others have become good managers of their reserves. And then there are those who have become a kind of romantic artifact that is pulled out for certain public events. Regardless of their personal characteristics, the Indigenous peoples of this place bear witness to another way of living. In their sufferings and in their joys, they know they belong here.

The Eyes of Newcomers and Outsiders

The garrison is now more of a metaphor than a reality. However, it endures as a default position, a reflex, and has now taken on diverse historical manifestations. It can be a default position for many countries and groups when they feel threatened and under attack. It can be a default position for groups and individuals who feel vulnerable and insecure. This defensiveness takes on an added determination when it is coupled with a colonial history of survival. Whenever or wherever a threat is perceived, there can be a cultural tendency to huddle together with others who are like us and help each other survive.

The shape and dynamic of our garrisons have varied from place to place in Canada and have taken on new characteristics in various historical periods. In the large metropolitan areas of Canada today, for example, ethnic groups cluster together in neighbourhoods with people like themselves. They support each other in the face of the daunting challenges of relating to the existing garrisons of interest and class. These communities of support and security are crucial … unless they also become defensive and isolating, places of exclusion.

The garrisons are now part of our history, but the garrison persists as a mentality whenever a threat, real or perceived, surfaces. Justice Thomas Berger has documented the various forms of exclusion that have shadowed the history of this country. In relatively peaceful times, he writes, Canada does seem to be a decent and tolerant country. Indeed, this is the way most Canadians think of themselves. However, he notes that tolerance and decency seem to evaporate in times of social and economic stress. The garrison mentality reappears in new forms. He cites the treatment of Jehovah's Witnesses in Quebec, the seizure of Doukhobor children in British Columbia, the internment of Japanese Canadians and the ex-clusion of Jewish refugees during the Second World War. He refers to the more recent invocation of the War Measures Act against a perceived insurrection in Quebec and the ongoing exclusion of Indigenous peoples. His book *Fragile Freedoms: Human Rights and Dissent in Canada* is aptly titled.

If Canada seems under threat today, it is no longer be-cause of the challenges posed by the natural world but because of the vast socio-economic forces unleashed by the process of globalization.

In the face of these threats, at the worst of times, we gather together with those like us and build walls. The walls are now invisible but real, constructed through papers and policies and subtle prejudices. In times of threat, our country becomes a garrison of garrisons, a collection of small and competing visions of the good. There have always been politicians and pundits who fuel this sense of fear and threat and divide groups from each other in the process.

It would be easy to blame this political protectionism on political leaders, but the best and the worst of the garrison mentality are within each of us. We can choose how we weigh in with our lives. I am concerned that we are defining our country by who/what we are against because we do not know what we are for. We do not know why we are here.

The ancient and wise ones and the newcomers have taught us how to see the countless ways in which we treat territorial Canada as a thing that we own, a thing that we possess and have a right to. We treat our natural resources as things that we own, and we treat the country as a place that we have a right to, where we can decide who gets in and who gets out. There is a national possessiveness that grips and possesses us as a nation.

Are We Possessed?

Nowhere is this more evident than in the North today. It is a place of great natural resources and awesome beauty, a vast space accessible to mining companies, the military and the few travellers who can afford it. The traders and tourists seldom meet the Indigenous peoples who live there and call it their homeland.

I was fortunate enough to spend some time in Nunavut and to see the world and my country from such a clear perspective. I saw a vast space that people from elsewhere wanted to possess and profit from. I saw the glaciers that were silently protecting the planet from climate change, the palaces of ice that were melting down from the effort. I saw a space that was silently serving the survival of all of us, a space for which we simply must commit ourselves to being responsible for.

For many of us, the North sits as some vast unconscious world of our more conscious lives to the South. It is a place of mystery still, not yet known. It is the frontier of a struggle that has been all too often repeated in the history of Canada. Strangers from another place have "discovered" the North and its resources. They begin to lease, to own, to buy and sell properties and rights. They treat the space of the North as if it were empty … They begin to "explore" the space and find relics from past explorations. The recently found ships from the Franklin expedition are not only historically significant but potentially significant in the political and legal dispute over who owns this place.

We want to possess this land, and we in turn are possessed. Until we learn to care for this land, we will not know how to work with it and with each other.

Fort McMurray exists as an open wound on the landscape of the North and in our souls. The resources are being gouged out of the earth and processed in a way that is pouring toxic waste into the water systems of the North. The natural resources have been sold to strangers who will never live on this land. And those who belong to the land are being driven away. Most Canadians have never seen Fort McMurray and the wreckage of the environment and a way of life. Nevertheless, many Canadians are benefiting from this massive project. It means jobs with good pay. The various levels of government are reaping the financial reward from the sale of this natural resource. Schools are being built on oil from the tar sands; hospitals are being upgraded; community centres are being funded. Good jobs are being created. Good people are working hard and supporting their families. No one can wash their hands clean of this oil.

If Canadians today were to cast a quick eye over the geography of our country, it is all too easy to say: We own this place. It is ours to barter and sell, ours to direct and defend, ours to appreciate and enjoy. We assume we have a right to be here. It seems sufficient to say that we are here to make a living. How thoughtlessly, how carelessly we live on this land and live from this land, yet we do not live within it.

One has only to listen to the very quiet ones, the ones still outside the garrisons of contempt, to know that we are a country riddled with social cruelty.

Our original sin remains with us, in us, as a defensive and sometimes destructive response to a real or perceived threat. It is not as obviously destructive as the furies that were unleashed on the American frontier, but it is just as real. Much depends on whether we think that our relationship with the Indigenous peoples and the natural world is permanently broken. Can this be repaired? Can this be redeemed? Do we have reason to hope?

The Truth and Reconciliation Commission stands as an essential point of reference back to our original moment as a country called Canada. It lays out the way back to the moments when the survival of the settlers was bought at the expense of the survival of the Indigenous peoples, to the moments when the garrisons were closed and cruel. They have a right to rage, long and loud.

The original sin will not easily be repaired. In our jagged history of first fearing nature and then managing it, we have lost our place. We have become builders and managers who have ventured out into the hinterland to harvest the natural resources. This history is not only a challenge but also an invitation for all of us to think, gratefully and carefully, about the natural world we live in, often without knowing it. It is a challenge to reimagine our relationship to the natural and human resources of this place, but one that we cannot and should not avoid as we begin to ask, "Why are we here?"

However, as long as the conversation continues along a well-beaten path, we will reach the dead-end question

"Who owns this land?" This question does not open up the way forward. It keeps us in our tragic illusion that we can or should or do possess this land.

How thoughtlessly we have become both producers and consumers of these "natural resources." We have become tourists driving through and beyond the beauty of the land. In the process we have become profoundly dislocated. We have tried to locate our national identity by talking about Canadian values, about the times when Canada defined itself by doing battle with foreign powers: Vimy, the Battle of Britain, the war in Afghanistan. The values are an abstraction, and the identity forged in battle, however noble and heroic, is an identity that relies on an enemy.

To find our way forward, we must go back to long ago – long before the Tsimshian chief.

4

Spacious
and Gracious

↔

The foundational experience of the early settlers has made it more difficult for us to answer the Tsimshian chief. We catch a glimpse of ourselves in moments of some collective effort to survive; we gather together to wait for the survivors of a disaster in the mines. We identify ourselves as a country that is rich in natural resources that we think we own and have a right to use. We define ourselves in terms of who or what we are against.

This leaves us with a very impoverished sense of why we are here: we have survived and so we will survive; we are making a living from our natural resources; we are not Americans or we are not Toronto!

Still, history lies heavy upon us. Residential schools. Japanese internment camps. Ships full of human misery that were prevented from docking: the *Komagata Maru*, the *St. Louis*, the *Ocean Lady* and the *Sun Sea*.

To see these realities is to see the real guilt we bear as a nation. This real guilt exposes the false innocence that we carefully cultivate as Canadians.

This is the beginning of living HERE in truth. However, it is not yet enough to sustain a positive sense of purpose. What are we here FOR?

Original Blessings

To respond to this question, we must draw on the reservoir of the original moment – not only the awareness of our original sin but also the reality of our original blessings.

I count it as a blessing that we live with a sense of the vastness of the world. This invites us, summons us, to find our appropriate place within this vastness: Do we want to dominate and control the immensity of the place we inhabit? Or do we feel overwhelmed and irrelevant by the sheer size and complexity of the place we call Canada? These are our questions today, just as they were the questions for the first settlers in this place.

Now, as then, the awareness of the immensity of the universe has coincided with the belief in a Creator. This was and is the wisdom of the Indigenous peoples. Again and again they refer to "the Creator" and to "Mother Earth." This was and is the wisdom of most of the world religions. "In the beginning, God created heaven and earth." These teachings have diverse variations, but there is a fundamental belief that the world was not constructed by human beings; it was a gift of the Creator.

It is because of this faith that we have the possibility of living within this vastness with a sense of awe and trust.

It is because of this faith that human beings knew they were neither the centre of the world nor irrelevant to its existence. The various myths attempt to describe how the world begins and is sustained. The fall and redemption of human beings is tied up with what they do with the world that is given to them. We fall when we begin to think we are the centre of the world, the makers of the world, the masters of the universe. We fall when we think we can manage this all.

We must acknowledge the immense wounds that have been inflicted by the settler cultures on the Indigenous peoples. However, and perhaps more importantly, we need to acknowledge and celebrate the wisdom of their understanding of this place on earth as a creation of the Creator. It is a wisdom that we need at this time and in this place.

This is the blessed wisdom which will help us to answer the question of the Tsimshian chief.

Many of the world religions (such as Judaism, Christianity and Islam) have crucial teachings around the notion of creation. Many of those teachings have lost their power as Western cultures celebrated the new world that human beings constructed and manufactured. In this new and modern world, human beings were at the centre of the universe: human beings had the right to own, to possess and to profit from this earth. In the process of improving the world, of making progress, the earth itself was taken for granted.

The great Czech playwright and president Vaclav Havel, who did not claim to be a Christian, was eloquent in his criticism of the Western secular tendency to place human beings in the centre of the world. He argued that the world needs to recentre itself, to remember that it is the creation of a transcendent mystery. This belief in a transcendent Creator, he said, was the only sure basis of world unity and the survival of the planet.

Those peoples and religions that acknowledge that the earth is a gift, never to be taken for granted, present a radical alternative to the carefully constructed and often violent Western ideal of progress. On the way to a better, richer, more exciting world, we have taken the earth itself for granted and have done much to damage it, if not destroy it.

We need to find our way back to an original moment so that we can find our true place and purpose in the world. We need to see the world as if on the first day of creation – so that we remember we are not the centre of the world, so we can take heart that this is not a world that we made or manufactured. In the morning of the world we awaken to the ground and the glimpse of goodness, to the mystery that grounds us and is given.

The Blessing Endures

There is a place for honest guilt, repentance and remembrance as we look backwards and then towards the future as a country that is now called Canada. Many in this country are now engaged in a sincere effort of truth and reconciliation with the Indigenous peoples of this country. This process is necessary. It will be long, hard and messy. It will not be perfect. It will not be sufficient.

However, we also need to draw on the sources of gratitude that reflect the kind of glee and excitement that newcomer kids have felt when they first encountered the vast wilderness of Canada. It is an attitude that the Tsimshian chief understood well – an attitude that the Indigenous peoples today have not forgotten. The attitude of gratitude. It means living with the simple awareness that the earth is not something that we human beings own or manufacture. The earth is a work of creation, a gift of the Creator. This means not taking the earth for granted. It means looking on this piece of earth, as if on the first day of creation, and seeing that it is indeed "very good."

To believe in the Creator is the deepest ground for believing in the power of limited human beings to create and recreate, to begin again, to begin anew. Fresh and free.

The Tsimshian chief was not marking his territory when he asked the question of the first settler. He was speaking as someone who felt responsible for the whole land. He was asking:

"What will you do for this (whole) place?"

The settlers assumed they had discovered this land, that no one else was here, at least no one of account, that they were the first and therefore had a right to it. The land was now their territory, something they possessed, an object to be used and disposed of. This presumptuous and possessive attitude was blessed by the representatives and leaders of the Christian churches.

Subsequent generations of settlers who came to define the outlines of the country that would be called Canada felt it was their right to cultivate, to improve the land, to mine its resources, to fix its problems, to build something better. And while this rush to progress and improvement was taking place, something was lost. The capacity for awe and gratitude. On the way to shaping a better country, we took the land, the water and the air for granted. We thought we knew what was best for this country. We thought we knew what was best for the Indigenous peoples. On the way to trying to make everything better, we lost sight of what was good in others, what was good in their "otherness." We lost sight of the good in ourselves.

We were not able to see that the Canada the settlers manufactured was worse than we thought.

And we were not able to see also that this Canada was better than we knew.

In our colonial blindness to what is HERE, we were unable to recognize what is special and unique and good HERE.

Too often we take Canada for granted. It is just there. It takes something of a political or climatic crisis for us to be shocked out of this insensitive and complacent attitude.

As individuals, we awaken each morning and take all this for granted. The alarm sounds, the coffee drips, the radio tells us what traffic and weather to expect, the breakfast is made – and we are off to work. We miss the amazing fact that we have indeed awakened and there is a world that is awakening, too. We take it for granted that there is an earth to stand on – an earth that holds us up and sustains us. We take the light and the air and the water for granted. And we take the people we care about and the ones we don't yet know for granted. We are so busy working for a living, improving our lives and those of others that we miss the amazing fact that there is a world to improve and people to care for. This daily miracle is worthy of our thanks. But our dominant culture teaches us to walk on by – especially if we have a cellphone and we are on it.

As citizens of this country, just like the Americans in theirs, we think that most problems can be solved if we just work hard enough and think smart enough. We are excited when Canada wins medals at the Olympics, when our scholars and writers receive recognition, when we are listed as one of the most liveable countries. But is that all there is?

We find it hard to answer the question of the Tsimshian chief because we can hardly hear it.

We're here because we're here because we're here... And so the campfire song goes.

There is noise and clutter and confusion and terminal busyness. If we could but stop to listen. What we need is here.

This is why it helps to see this place with fresh eyes, with the eyes of the newcomers, the children who glisten with glee and gratitude. If the newcomer refugee adults were asked by the Tsimshian chief, "Why are you here?" most of them would begin by answering, "*We are here to survive.*" They have fled from places where the weight of history, the clash of political realities or the crush of poverty made it impossible for them to survive there.

These newcomers arrive in a place that seems much less weighted by history and violence. In time they will discover our particular forms of social cruelty, but the first impression is significant. They understand that this is a place with a relatively short history. There are the sins of the past, but they seem less heavy, less intractable. This is a place where you could find shelter, a home, even if you never owned a house. *What we need is here.* This is a place that is big and cold, but it also warms with a future, a promised land where new things seem possible. It is a blessed place.

It is bestowed. It cannot be bought or sold. *It is more than enough.*

As I consider Canada as a whole, thoughtfully, prayerfully, it seems like such a vastness. I think this is what the refugee children saw as they flew off the cliff into Horseshoe Lake. This is a place where there is room for what is new, for the people who are new. Even the harsh and cold winters seem to hold the promise of spring and new life. This is a place where something new is possible, a new way of being, a new way of acting. And this is true even in urban areas… There is still room here. There is still the possibility of renewal. The size and space of the country is not only geographic; it can also become an act of imagination and a way of freedom. It can also become a mindset, a way of feeling, seeing and giving.

Still, the long, cold shoulder in Canada can make various immigrant groups huddle together to create some space of sureness within the large metropolitan areas and in the somewhat invisible social fabric of the country. Refugees and immigrants are not perfect people, just as Indigenous peoples are not perfect. They can be as obstinate and short-sighted as anyone else. However, people do not need to be perfect in order to speak truly, in order to get justice, in order to be good.

Gatherings of Giving

There are times and places when we all come out of our garrisons and greet each other, welcome each other. For example, every Christmas Day, Romero House holds an Evening of Peace that is open to any and all people regardless of religion, culture or race. The only recommendation is that each guest bring some contribution of food or drink. Many will get up and sing or dance to some rhythm from another place. Some evenings there will be over 200 people there, many of them strangers to each other from various communities in the city. Invariably, I will hear one of the guests say to another almost complete stranger, "Isn't this amazing? We can be together in peace."

I have seen a similar sense of peace during the potluck suppers for Writers in Exile, sponsored by PEN Canada. As I have reflected on these suppers, I have come to the conclusion that they work because they are potluck. The suppers are an opportunity for each person to contribute to the well-being of all. No matter what food or drink someone brings, it is an expression of our capacity to give something to others, to share a responsibility for a good gathering. I believe that our future as a country will depend on developing social forms in which people will be encouraged to contribute to the common good. Our first question to the newcomer should not be "What have you come to take?" The first question should be "What do you have to offer?"

I have also learned to see this country from the perspective of a mother from Africa who walked across the Peace Bridge between Canada and the United States. She walked with nothing but her five little children and an overnight bag. She had arrived on a plane from Africa and landed in New York City, where she got a bus to Buffalo and then a taxi to the bridge to Canada.

She walked over that bridge not knowing anyone or anything that was on the other side. She was bringing her hope to this country. She was offering her hope in a good and just country to us Canadians. We must learn to see our country with such hope, just as we must learn to see the shadows of the past.

I think she would have been welcomed by the Tsimshian chief. He would understand her hope. He would say, "*We have room enough for hope.*"

For this woman and these children, and for countless others over the past two hundred years, this place has offered the possibility of a new beginning.

So we are challenged and invited by both the most ancient ones and the newcomers to see this place as if for the first time, as if in the beginning, through a wrinkle in time. With awe, astonishment and gratitude. Many Canadians have been settled here for some time. Among these settlers are those who have really lived HERE; others who are still on the way to someplace else. Those who have really lived HERE have seen with their own eyes and have, from time to time, been astonished by this place.

We can all begin by seeing the earth as a small planet within an immense cosmos – a vastness, a spaciousness. The earth is small but not insignificant.

Each one of us can begin to wonder where we belong in such vast spaciousness. In different locations, the first settlers encountered this vastness in the rivers, the forests, the oceans and the length of sky over the plains. We have learned that the first settlers felt afraid and overwhelmed by this vast and threatening land. We know they built structures and communities to survive in the face of this threat. We know they excluded the strangers who were associated with this threat. These first settlers felt diminished by the vastness of this place and yet they did not disappear. In their determination not to disappear, they engaged in a process of the disappearance of the Indigenous peoples and the destruction of large areas of the natural world. All in the name of survival.

Beyond Fear and the Desire to Control

Yet, these early settlers did not seek to dominate and destroy the wilderness around them. Not totally. Not completely. Unlike the Americans to the south, the settlers arriving in Canada did not seek to become the masters of the universe. But what did they, and we, seek to become? Now we must ask ourselves the lengthening question of the Tsimshian chief. How do we want to relate to this particular place on earth and to the people who were the original inhabitants?

It would be folly to believe the contemporary struggle for Canadians is to become first in the order of things. It would be tragic if we made the assessment that our vast natural resources could be the ticket to power and richness. It would be short-sighted if we saw the vast natural and human resources in our multicultural society as a ticket to mastering the global economy.

Our struggle should not be to become a great power. As I suggested previously, it should be a struggle to find our right place, which is neither at the bottom nor at the top of the order of the universe. We must search for a true place, a good place, a place in which we will know for sure that we Canadians are not the centre of the world, yet we are occupying a place from which we can measure our lives against a vast horizon of hope and expectation.

We need to find our place in this vastness – beyond fear but also beyond the desperate illusion that we can and should control this vastness. There are other cultures, with a long history and a smaller geography that feel crowded and restricted, where the struggle to find one's place becomes more complex, more interior. However, those who live in Canada face daily reminders of the size and shape of their lives in the face of a geographic vastness and almost constant reminders of an immense variety of cultures and the immense scope of human achievements. We are struggling to find our place in this vastness, this spaciousness which challenges and invites us to nothing less than a spiritual spaciousness.

One would think that this vast spaciousness would incline us to welcome people to this place, as there is indeed room enough for hope and for so many more people. However, we know from our history that this vastness can quickly stimulate an amorphous sense of threat: the garrisons are rebuilt or relocated and the strangers are excluded.

How else can we understand the amazing fluctuations in our attitudes towards the strangers and newcomers? At times we know in our hearts and minds that we have room in this place, and at other times we are fearful, small-minded and mean-hearted.

In a time of vast globalization, many are reacting by putting down roots in a more local situation. Thus, we have a new surge of energy and commitment to local forms of governance, to local economies and local communities. This is where people put down roots as a counterweight to the forces of globalization. One can have an affection for such local realities, but loyalty and affection for something as abstract as "the earth" is much harder to realize.

Loyalty and affection are always local. I sense that for each Canadian, there are one or two or a few places that locate our affection for Canada: the street where we live, the school where we teach, the team that needs and deserves our loyalty. Thus, it seems rather hollow to say that we "love" Canada, that very big place on the map. The refugee who climbed to the promontory overlooking the North Channel and Manitoulin Island was not shouting his love to the whole of the contemporary nation. He was proclaiming his love for what he could see and sense.

Canada is too big to "love." However, it can be imagined with gratitude; it can be inhabited with a sense of responsibility.

The landscape, whether urban or rural or bush country, lies before us … around us … and we often treat it as an object. As though it is something that we own, something that is ours, a possession that we seek to control. It is not something that we are part of. We drive through it like a tourist.

For each of us there is the challenge of finding our place. For us to become a city, a village, we must find our place. For us as a country, we may be on the cusp of finding our true place in the world.

If there is such a thing as social conversion, it would mean a change in us as a people: from taking this place for granted to treating it with a sense of gratitude. Gratitude may be the ground of a new sensibility, a new sense of responsibility to and for the earth.

A social conversion would mean challenging and changing our colonial consciousness that has been formed over the centuries. It would mean changing our relationship to the American empire so that we can learn to think and imagine, act and pray, with a sense of gratitude and responsibility for who and what is HERE.

Such a conversion could mean allowing ourselves to admit that the American empire is in decline, realizing that the new Republicans are withdrawing into their own garrison and manufacturing "enemies" as a way of uniting the American people against the world. It would also mean refusing to transfer our colonial mindset to another empire, such as the Chinese empire. It would mean becoming a good and substantial country instead of a colony in a great empire.

Let me return to the two stories I referred to earlier in order to frame an answer to the question of the Tsimshian chief. It should now be apparent that they suggest that what we hold in common as a country is the space that we inhabit.

If we pay attention to the geography of this place called Canada, we must acknowledge the obvious: it is a place marked out by a border. This border or boundary is shaped partly by geography but mostly by the events of history. The borders exist and they are important, but there is nothing sacred about these boundaries. They are not God given. Too many wars have been fought in the name of thoughtless, careless nationalism.

Nevertheless, how we think about these borders may be our greatest challenge and our greatest gift that we as a country have to give to the world: a spaciousness of spirit that is gracious.

5

Grounds for Responsibility

↔

I t makes a difference whether gratitude or posses-siveness is the fundamental attitude that animates a social or political entity. Neither attitude auto-matically implies a certain public policy or legislation. It is possible, for example, to believe that a sense of gratitude will lead to a wider sense of social sharing. It is also possible to think that gratitude for what is given will lead to a deeper sense of wanting to protect and conserve what has been given. Nevertheless, it does make a difference in the most subtle and fundamental ways.

Gratitude and Power

If we believe that we possess a society or a country, we will take great care to protect our rights and, possibly, the rights of others. If, on the other hand, a social group is sustained by a sense of gratitude for what has been given, then it will want to enhance the scope of that gratitude in the world and to give back. Gratitude as a social attitude is the deepest ground for a sense of responsibility. It is when we accept Canada as a gift that we want to give back to this country, freely and hap-pily, and to give from this country to those in greatest need.

67

Citizenship is then a grateful responsibility. It is not a sort of share in the ownership of the country; it is a gift that we receive in the sharing of it. Possessive nationalism measures itself in terms of greatness; grateful responsibility, by way of contrast, guides the vision of becoming a good country by living in cooperation. I am not referring to responsibility as some grim sense of obligation. I am suggesting that kind of responsibility that arises as a response from a sense of gratitude and carries the possibility of a more spacious sense of sharing.

However, I want to acknowledge that the goal of becoming a good country can seem rather naïve and even powerless in the face of the power exercised by the dominant powers of the world, by the controlling interests in the very big global economy. Does this mean that we will remain a nice country, a cautious garrison in the face of the powers of the world? How long will we hesitate?

Faced with the question of the Tsimshian chief we may answer: *We really don't know why we are here, and we are not sure we want to know.*

Answering the question of the Tsimshian chief honestly would require cleansing our minds and hearts of the spiritual and political afflictions of consumerism and a history of colonialism. It would mean reconsidering our debilitating view of power and searching for a more creative and constructive sense of power that would allow us to take the chief's question seriously.

Imperial Power

Our history, like that of other nations, reflects the dynamics of power that have long shaped the world. We know what imperial power means because we have seen it and felt it from the perspective of a colony. We have seen how it constructs a colony and keeps it under control: it means the power to control a place, its resources and a people. It means the capacity to control through economic power, political power, military might and even violence. Power can be mean and ugly. It can crush all alternatives in its wake. It can also evoke a sense of awe, fear and reverence in some people. This is the power of empire: sometimes more subtle and sometimes more obvious. This kind of power is something to be feared, resented or even desired.

The Power of Knowledge and Technology

This kind of controlling power has been increasingly and inevitably associated in modern times with the acquisition of knowledge and information and with the inventions of technology. This modern version of how the world can be and should be changed has shaped America more than any-place else on earth. It fed the vision of progress that gave early European settlers in Canada (and elsewhere) the conviction that they could and should take charge of the natural world through the inventions of technology – railways, heavy equipment for fishing the oceans, and machinery for harvesting grain, cutting trees and mining the earth.

Astonishment and awe, faith and trust, and hope beyond reason were consigned to those who had not yet learned how the world worked. The world was seen as an object, a machine, that could be analyzed, broken down into component parts and reconstructed in better ways. So, too, human beings were seen as the objects of research to be catalogued and rehabilitated – either psychologically or sociologically.

The power of technology enabled the European settlers in 18th- and 19th-century Canada to overcome their fear of the natural world, to tame it, to use it for profit. Coupled with this effort was the effort to tame the Indigenous peoples, to make them more efficient and to assimilate them in the name of progress. The plains were cleared of the people who had lived there for centuries to make room for the great railway that would link east to west.

The Centre and Periphery of Power

The power of empire, whether French or British or American, harnessed the power of technology and made the area known as Canada a vast hinterland that served the interests of the metropolitan areas of the imperial powers. Within the hinterland of Canada there were lesser metropolitan cities that simultaneously controlled that hinterland while being controlled by the head offices in the capitals of empire.

It is possible to review the history of Canada and to learn how power exercised at the centre of this country affected the lives of those who live on the periphery or in the hinterland. Canada became both the victim and the perpetrator of various forms of colonialism. The business elites have controlled the lives of people in the regions (the West, the Maritimes, the North) and the lives of those in the periphery of poverty in large cities. The result is that most Canadians, whether they live in the hinterland or the metropolis, think they have relatively little power to control their own lives. They believe the most important decisions affecting their lives are made in the head office, which is always someplace else.

There are centres of controlling power in Canada and there are victims of that kind of power. This sense of controlling power and the sense of powerlessness are closely intertwined. If we think that having power means being totally in control, then this perception generates a sense of being completely powerless. It seems we can sometimes prefer the innocence that comes with this sense of powerlessness. It may make us feel less guilty, but it also leaves us with a sense of the insignificance of our own actions.

"*Why are you here?*" asks the chief.

I was sent by someone else – a government, a church, a company.

The Power to Be Responsible

If we do not believe we have the power to do wrong, we will not be convinced that we have the power to do right. Our actions will lack seriousness. Without a sense of power, we will not have a sense of the significance of our lives and actions. Without a sense of power, we can never become responsible.

If we believe we are fundamentally powerless to shape our own reality as a country, then we will act and speak and decide in ways that will ensure that we will remain powerless. If, in spite of our proud rhetoric and more conspicuous nationalism, we remain deep down sure that we are controlled by an imperial power or global corporation, we will indeed remain a colony. We may give bold and beautiful statements at the United Nations that lack the power to persuade – not only because of the obduracy of others, but also because we have not persuaded ourselves. Powerlessness is a self-fulfilling prophecy.

A country that has a foundational experience of being a colony faces at some point the challenge of how to deal with imperial, controlling and coercive power.

At some point, and that point is now, we need to reflect on what kind of power we want and need if we are to live with gratitude and responsibility for the place called Canada.

At some point, and that point is now, we begin to reshape our relationship with America through various trade negotiations.

71

The Decline of the American Empire

Empires past and present define themselves as the centre of the world and the rest of the world only in reference to this centre. It creates, in peoples and individuals, what I would call "the Imperial Self" that thinks itself, for better or worse, to be the centre of the world.

America has been the engine of global consumerism, but it is no longer the centre of the world. It continues to exist as an important point of reference because of its military power, but it is no longer the economic or political centre of the world. The most powerful nation on earth, our closest "friend and ally," has been thrown off centre. Many Americans, rich, poor and middle-class, are now experiencing a spiritual crisis, a crisis of identity because they no longer have the power to control the world or to lead it. Either you are in control or you are not. The depth of this dislocation cannot be underestimated. This spiritual crisis of meaning and purpose is now being deeply felt in Canada. We, too, feel a sense of dislocation. It is a moment to ask, "*Where is here? Why are we here?*"

Will we search for another empire to belong to? Will another empire come along to take us over?

Perhaps we have reached the moment, our first genuinely post-colonial moment, when we can begin to begin HERE. Perhaps we have reached the point when we are ready to be responsible for HERE and for NOW.

All empires decline, and they are dangerous in the process of following this inevitable trajectory. A loss of a common overarching vision is the deepest sign of this process of decline. Empires in a state of development are drawn together and drawn forward by an overarching vision that is shared by its peoples. The dimming of that vision coincides with a loss of economic and political power.

When this happens, an empire begins to define itself more in terms of what it is against than what it is for. Something like this happened in America after the Second World War. America no longer defined itself as The City on the Hill that was a beacon for the values of democracy. In the early 1950s, America began to define itself as being AGAINST Communism. And when that great enemy fell, then it manufactured other enemies such as Noriega, Saddam Hussein, the Taliban and "the terrorists." America is now acting like a garrison, turning inward in the face of threat. "America first!" is a defensive assertion, not a creative one.

Watching the brutal exercise of power that advances empires, those who live in an empire's colonies are tempted to seek some form of countervailing power that offers liberation from this controlling power... but also presents new dangers. In this process, with no vision of our own, we can become like that which we are fighting against.

Colonized peoples can also prefer to remain innocent and powerless. They do not want the sense of guilt and responsibility that comes from exercising power. They place the responsibility for the important decisions (affecting the economy, public policy and social justice) with the head office, which is always ELSEWHERE and never here.

It also prevents us from exercising the very real power that we do have: the power not only to do wrong but to do what is right and good. Tommy Douglas became the father of Medicare in Canada because he conveyed a sense of moral power that convinced people they could do something fresh and new. Saskatchewan, the dustbowl of the prairies, became the incubator for one of the boldest political initiatives in all of North America.

We can also recall when Gander, Newfoundland, welcomed hundreds of passengers who were grounded in the

73

days after 9/11. Together, the people of Gander said not only "We should do this" but "We can do this." We also remember how the country reached out to welcome thousands of Syrian refugees.

Are we then caught between a controlling exercise of power and a helpless and dangerous sense of innocence? Yes, if we accept that this is the only way of considering power. Much of our political and social theory is based on a concept of power that is a commodity that a few people have a lot of and many people have little of. It cannot easily be divided or shared, and various constitutional arrangements exist to balance different powers within a nation or a global organization.

Creative Power/Cooperative Power

However, there are other ways of looking at power that are important for any person or group intuiting that they have something significant to say, who want to change the world for the better. The contemporary insight (actually, it is very old as well) that power is an energy more than a thing has enormous implications for science and for social and political theory about how human beings can organize themselves to make a difference.

Contemporary science, such as quantum physics, has given us new insight into an older and static view of the world, namely that things and beings are connected in a network of energy and life. Electrical power, for example, arises from the interaction of two poles. It is not generated by only one pole. Nuclear power and solar power are generated by the interaction of various components. Human power is also generated in the process of social and political interaction. Thus, we see important examples of groups of people who made a difference out of all proportion to their economic resources, the size of their military, the numbers of their peoples.

This is the bright side of what the early settlers learned during their foundational experience within the garrisons: that they could not only survive but also flourish together. They learned the value of interaction and cooperation. They also learned this from the Indigenous peoples who were willing to help them. We have an ancient memory that the Indigenous peoples taught us to honour: that we live first not as individuals but as members of a community.

This sense of the power that is generated through interaction is crucial if we are to begin to answer the question of the Tsimshian chief. If we cannot take ourselves seriously as agents of change, we will take for granted our place in the world, until we believe that we have the power to do something significant in this time and place.

To accept and then confirm a sense of interactive power will enable us to move beyond our protective enclaves, defined rather pathetically by who and what we are against. There are indeed garrisons within our Canadian garrisons: many Québécois against English Canada; the West against the East, the North against the South, the rural areas against the big cities, environmentalists against Big Oil, developers against the homeless, the whole country against Toronto. And the whole country against the United States.

This negative definition of power works – and only sort of – for just a while. It can fuel election campaigns and generate material for a great deal of comedy. Yet, it is a sad sign when a country has to define itself mainly by who and what it is against. It usually means it does not know who and what it is FOR.

America is gripped by a politics of division in which a variety of groups have defined themselves in terms of what they are AGAINST. Indeed, the post-American century is now redrawing the global map in terms of who and what

America is against. It makes it all the more difficult, and all the more necessary, to claim some sense of a positive vision and purpose.

To begin to see where here is would be to release ourselves from our image of ourselves as a lesser reality, a smaller power attached to a "great" empire. It would mean, among many things, to begin seeing the good that is here and the power for good (and ill) that is ours to live out.

We are not masters, nor are we only survivors: we have the possibility of learning how to live within the vast space that we call Canada, of finding our place – which is neither above nor below but WITHIN it. We would need to choose to become not a great nation but a good nation. It would mean choosing to build a future not just on guilt but on gratitude, to be responsible not only for our past but for our future and our present place in this world.

We can and must interact with the Indigenous peoples of this place. We can and must discover together our resources for the energy of creative power. We can and must together begin again. This is the task of truth and reconciliation: acknowledging the way that all settlers in this country, consciously or unconsciously, exercised power in a controlling and imperial way. Acknowledging our false innocence. Believing and hoping, beyond reason, that together we can and must begin again to create a good place on this earth.

To believe in the Creator is to believe in the possibility of human beings beginning again. To believe in the Creator means to acknowledge that we are creatures with the limited but real possibility of being creative. To acknowledge our true place as creatures is to hope in the possibility of beginning again, in the reality of redemption.

6

What Are We For?

⟵✦⟶

L et me return to the two stories that have framed the reflections in this meditation. The story of the little urban street describes how very diverse people can feel responsible for a common space that is concrete and is recognized as a common good. The story of the refugee children seeing the Canadian wilderness for the first time reveals how seeing nature with new eyes indicates the good that we hold in common as a nation. We hold this land in common.

Describing the Common Good

The common good is a rather ancient notion in the Western tradition of social and political thought. Interestingly enough, it is a concept that is rarely defined in detail, although it exists as an essential point of reference. There are those thinkers who have been rightly wary of any attempt to define this notion because it easily became associated with the attempts of one group or another to presume the authority to define what was right and good for everyone. In other words, the notion of the common good could be used to justify oppressive uniformity, rigid orthodoxy and imperial sameness.

Nevertheless, the notion of the common good persists because it inspires, encourages and appeals to what is good in us – not merely as individuals, but as citizens and members of society. It draws us forward with a sense of the good that we are FOR rather than what we are against. It acts as an important alternative to a significant strain of modern political thought that is based on social views constituted by the primacy of individual rights and possessions, private property and personal achievement. Such is the liberal democratic form of politics in which the role of government is not so much to define or support the common good as to facilitate the interaction of various individual and group interests so that there will be the greatest good for the greatest number of people. This liberal political view of government parallels the economic view that the market will be guided by an invisible hand that will manage various competing interests so that the greatest profit may result for the greatest number of people.

There is no compelling or shared vision in this form of possessive politics and economics. It is based on the simple belief that there will be more and more for more and more people if we simply work harder and think smarter. There is really not much to unify a country from such a political perspective. A government may manage the conflicts of competing interests, but it will not draw diverse people together to cooperate in a spirit of sacrifice for a greater good.

The notion of the common good developed during the classical and medieval periods in Europe. Then, as now, the notion was barely defined, although it was much referred to. My sense is that it did not need to be defined because people understood what it meant in the course of their daily experience of the space they lived in. Within the small villages, the monasteries and the feudal lands of medieval times, most communities had an area called "the commons." This space was used in many ways: it was a place to trade, a place to celebrate weddings and other social events, a place for tournaments, a place for animals to graze and for meetings to be held. *It was a place that no one owned but everyone could use and be responsible for.* Medieval thinkers did not have to define the common good because people lived within it as part of their daily reality.

It was a public space that gradually disappeared as more and more of the space was enclosed and more and more became private property in the 18th century. Today, there is a renewed interest in the space that could be described as "the commons". The term is understood to describe a very large or very small space that is held in common. Some ecological theories describe the whole earth as the good that we most hold in common. Educational institutions use the term "Information commons" to describe the shared responsibility of libraries, cultural institutions, centres of learning and research. Local information, local politics and local economics have emerged as ways of energizing responsibility for the location of the common good.

A Very Big Responsibility

There is a growing awareness that we are all living in one world. Through economics and technology, our future is inextricably linked with the fate of the earth that we all share. The concern over climate change is based on an intense awareness that we live in a global ecosystem that knows no borders. Waste and garbage and pollution know no boundaries. We all live downstream, as the saying goes. The threat of nuclear war binds all countries together in fear. Indeed, it is now more urgent than ever to affirm that the earth is the primary good that we all hold in common. We are slowly working our way towards the political and economic structures that will support this big-picture affirmation.

Between the Local and the Global

Nevertheless, care for the earth is a vast concern: so vast that it can leave us feeling powerless, can turn us towards focusing on the local realities that we think we can do something about. The concern for local realities and working on environmental issues as a local commitment is significant and important. The prophetic voice of Wendell Berry has reminded us that we only think well and carefully when we are rooted in a very particular place. Once our thinking becomes too large and abstract, our view becomes careless and can even become destructive.

Our most serious political question now is the role of various intermediate political bodies, such as bioregions and free trade zones, that are situated somewhere between the local and the global. Many nation-states are under increasing stress, situated in a world where power is being drawn upwards towards a more global concern and downwards towards more local commitments.

A country such as Canada seems to have little control over the forces of globalization that are weakening our ability to make decisions within our national borders. And the nation seems less able to engage the sense of commitment and affection that is experienced by people at the local level: whether in a small urban neighbourhood, a local school, a small farm, or a craft brewery or winery. To me, efforts to construct a sense of national identity and purpose out of a shared sense of history, common values or a common culture are not going to fulfill this great expectation. This is why we need to find a new appreciation for the role of nation-states in which citizens can take responsibility not for the whole earth, but for a significant and meaningful part of that earth.

Borders as the Delineation of Responsibility

What would it mean to become a good country: a country with a sense of the common good? The preceding reflections suggest that it would mean organizing our social and public priorities around a common good that none of us own but all of us are responsible for. *For starters, let us say that in Canada, the good we now hold in common is the geography delineated by our national boundaries.* This is the place on earth that we can enjoy, benefit from and care for. This is the place where we can begin to develop appropriate social forms of responsibility.

The first settlers in this place were frightened by the vast space that surrounded them. It both threatened to engulf them and offered great promise. Subsequent generations of newcomers overcame this fear and realized the promise through the use of knowledge and technology and mutual respect. Our challenge now is whether we can or do relate to the vastness of this land beyond fear, beyond indifference. Can we be summoned by the vastness of this land to a sense of care and responsibility?

To think this way would mean reimagining the borders of Canada in terms of who and what we are for   not in terms of some real or imagined threat. Our borders have been drawn for reasons of geography and history. These borders are sometimes artificial: they cut across some natural bioregions and ignore the homeland areas of the Indigenous peoples. But here they are. They are not God-given and they are not forever. But for now, they exist as the borders of the country called Canada.

Depending on how we see the country, we will treat these borders as barriers to protect what we think we own and possess as a country, or we will appreciate these boundaries anew as the delineation of our sphere of responsibility for this earth.

Why are we here? We are here to take up responsibility for this place on earth, for the sake of the whole earth.

Through the eyes of the Tsimshian chief and through the eyes of refugees and good neighbours, I have seen that we do have a common good in Canada, a good that is so obvious it is elusive. We hold this place in common. How we hold this place in common, the fundamental attitudes we bring to this task, are linked to our sense of why we are here. We are here to take up our responsibility for this place on earth.

If we cast our eyes across and around the geographical area defined as Canada by borders, we see vast urban geography of small towns and large urban areas in which a sense of the commons is played out in real and exciting ways. We see vast areas of the North, that mysterious canvas on which settlers have painted their own projections and illusions. The place that is a homeland for Indigenous peoples and the creatures of the North. We have great lakes and small lakes (nearly two million!) and waterways, immense by any standards. And there is a vast underground of minerals and liquid energy.

This place is the good that we hold in common. It relies on a sense of responsibility for what is held in common, which no one owns but all are responsible for. The sense of the common good relies much more on a sense of responsibility than on claims to rights.

Some of our most intense conflicts at the moment are over who holds the rights to natural resources such as oil, gas, minerals, water, trees: Is it the federal government, the provincial government, the Indigenous peoples? Such conflicts seem to intensify with the passage of time and are not easily resolved through negotiation or litigation. Perhaps it is time to begin by asking another question: Who is willing to take up responsibility for these resources? I am convinced that if we take up this challenge with an urgent sense of responsibility, we will find the basis for a renewed sense of neighbourliness and a new commitment to citizenship.

Our bitter conflicts within this country arise from the possessiveness that infects our political and economic lives: Who owns this? Who owns that? Such debates leave us exhausted and demoralized, unable to sustain a vast care for this land.

The greatest requirement for taking HERE to heart and mind is that we do not take this place for granted. All too often we cannot see the ground beneath our feet; we take for granted the way it holds us up and surrounds us. We know our country, but only numbly so.

We are Canadians because we inhabit a particular place on earth that is defined by national borders. We take this, too, for granted. What a liberation it would be to pay attention to where we are, to be astonished by the gift of living in this particular place on earth.

To sustain a care for this whole land, we need to be able to imagine the boundaries of our concern, the delineation of care marked out by our geographic boundaries. And we need to find like-spirited people with whom we can gather to sustain our vast care and concern.

Communities of Responsibility

Long ago, the settlers constructed garrisons to ensure their survival against vast threats. Today we need to construct communities of responsibility that will ensure the survival of our care and commitment. Survival is a complex process. It involves two choices: the first is the choice not to die, and the second is the choice to live.

Canadians today need to gather together with like-spirited people who bear a sense of responsibility for this vast land.

This meditation is only the beginning. It is meant to awaken the desire to be responsible for the common good in and of Canada. How that can be realized will be the practical and political challenge of these times. It will not be easy. Success is not a sure thing. But it will be a challenge worthy of our lives.

This meditation does suggest that certain groups must be included in this task: we need the wisdom and courage of Indigenous peoples, the excitement of newcomers and the energy of young people. These are the people who know how to say thank you. These are the ones who need only the possibility of contributing something significant to this country.

Nevertheless, each one of us has the potential to become part of the answer to the question of the Tsimshian chief. Each one of us – young or old, Indigenous or settler, rich or poor, self-taught or formally educated, musicians and mathematicians – can make a difference.

It makes all the difference in the world whether we take this country for granted or see it as a gift.

It makes a difference whether we see the earth as an object that we have the right to own, possess and use, or we see the earth as the place we inhabit and have a responsibility for.

It makes a difference in public policy, economic and social priorities and environmental awareness.

It makes a difference in how we see our national borders in relationship to the good we hold in common.

What would it mean if we treated this country not so much as a possession or even as an achievement, but as a promise to be fulfilled?

The next few generations will be about finding our true place in the world. Not as peacekeepers in some distant places, not as some soft middle power, not as a storehouse of natural resources to be bought and sold. Our future depends on a profound shift in our attitude towards the place on earth that we inhabit. It will mean refusing to treat this place as some chunk of earth that we own, that we can sell and buy back and profit from. This kind of possessive nationalism lies at the basis of the arrogant assumption that we own this place, that we have the right to decide who gets in and who stays out.

This does not mean that we should all go into the wilderness and hug the trees, nor does it mean we should all go to powwows or stand at the dock or the airport, waving in the refugees. It would mean cultivating the imagination of seeing our rural areas, our towns and villages, our wilderness and our metropolitan areas as linked together in a network of interdependency. We need to think of our large cities as "natural cities" within the larger geography of the country. Cities do not have the right simply to use the natural resources they need: air, water, oil and gas, wood, food. Cities have the responsibility to care for the resources they need. This is the art of the commonplace.

We have a responsibility to re-vision our cities as habitations within a larger ecosystem, as natural cities that are habitations rather than garrisons protecting us from each other and from the natural world. We need to imagine those spaces within cities and towns where people can exercise responsibility for places in which the common good is obvious and tangible.

In a time of global climate change, our responsibility for the environment we live in takes on particular significance. It matters to the whole earth, to other nations whose ecosystems are closely linked to ours. "This," as Naomi Klein has written, "changes everything." We have almost two million freshwater lakes in Canada. And this in a world where drought is a daily reality for many. And this in a country where those who live on reserves have to beg for clean drinking water.

When I visited the awesomely beautiful Arctic – which is largely our responsibility – on a study tour in 2013, we could see the glaciers breaking apart and falling into the waters as we went past the icebergs in our little boats. The polar icecap on Greenland is rapidly melting. Climate change is real. What is happening in the North has implications for all people throughout the world. Meanwhile, several nations are fighting over who has the right to the natural resources in the area. The conversation remains dangerously and recklessly and tediously about "Who owns the Arctic?" rather than "Who will take responsibility for the Arctic?"

People in the South are discussing this situation, but up North and far away in the Arctic are small villages of Inuit. Researchers in remote field stations are measuring the ice in the dark days of winter. They are issuing a prophetic message: the ice is melting and the whole earth will be affected. One does not need to go north to see what our northern neighbours are telling us. This is not only their responsibility. What is happening in the Arctic is a responsibility we all share.

We must look at how we in the South are living: our way of being, our economies that depend on the profits and taxes made from the Arctic's natural resources. We must, right where we are, take on the weight of the space we inhabit. We must embrace the political responsibility for the natural resources of air and water, the Arctic climate, the forests that breathe oxygen into the air, the topsoil in the fertile South that has taken thousands of years to build.

Each one of us – individuals, companies and organizations – can and must assume this responsibility for Canada in different ways. We will still need to discuss and debate our national priorities, our public policy. We will argue and disagree, but we might begin to respect and care for the good that we hold in common.

This much is still possible: If we take on, consciously and together, active care for this particular place on earth, then we will discover what holds the immense diversity of this country together. We hold a street in common, a neighbourhood, a city, a village, a park, a vastness... We are not owners but inhabitants of this place.

We are inhabitants. *Les habitants.*

Why are you here?

Here I am. Here we are.

Acknowledgements

These reflections are part of a longer and deeper effort to live here, in the place called Canada. Through my involvement in PEN Canada, particularly the Writers in Exile Supper Club, I have learned a great deal from writers who "come from away" and see this country in new and fresh ways. I have also learned to see through the eyes of the refugees I have lived with at Romero House in Toronto. I am grateful to all the members of the Romero House community who have helped me to see and to listen to the cadences of this country.

I am also thankful for my long and ordinary friendship with Beverly Keeshig-Soonias, who invited me to walk back along ancient paths in the hope of discovering a new way.

My indebtedness to many Canadian writers and thinkers will be evident in the endnotes for each chapter of this book.

Thanks to the faculty and students of the Toronto School of Theology (particularly Regis College) and to the Oblate School of Theology in San Antonio, who welcomed my efforts to think about the Canadian context. In particular, I thank my academic colleagues who were generous with their time and attention to these reflections when they were still inchoate and undeveloped: Gregory Baum, Margaret Brennan IHM, Douglas Hall, Stephen Scharper and Hilary Cunningham,

Mary Ann Hinsdale IHM and Marilyn Legge. Michael Creal gathered a discussion group on Canadian theology more than 25 years ago. The monthly conversation included David Clark and Floyd Honey and was a source of inspiration. Michael Valpy, journalist and serious citizen, was particularly helpful in discussing the insights that shape these reflections. Anna Porter, writer and publisher, was wise and encouraging in her comments on the early drafts of this book. I am grateful to Bertha Yetman and the insight in her doctoral thesis that the crisis of the cod fishery in Newfoundland was a crisis of the common good. Jack Costello SJ helped me to refine these reflections throughout the long process of writing them down.

I am grateful to the Canada Council for the generous grant that made it possible for me to travel to the Arctic on a study tour in the summer of 2013. My sister, Jennifer Leddy, was profoundly impressed by the Arctic on that trip and shared that keen interest with me as she described her subsequent trips to the far North.

Joe Sinasac, Simon Appolloni and Anne Louise Mahoney of Novalis Publishing were very patient and helpful throughout the publication process. As always, I am grateful to my agent, Lee Davis Creal, for her wise advice and practical assistance.

Chris Lind, a colleague and friend, believed passionately in the importance of taking the context of Canada not only to heart but also to the soul and the mind. He convened a wonderful group of people to a three-day seminar (February 15-17, 2013) at the Sorrento Retreat Centre in the beautiful Shuswap region of British Columbia. We discussed the first draft of these reflections in what was called "the first Sorrento Seminar." Chris died of brain cancer shortly after that gathering. My hope is that these reflections carry his convictions and concerns forward.

Endnotes

In an effort to ensure a more meditative tone in the text of these reflections, I have tried to sustain some simple insights which can lead to further considerations. The endnotes to each chapter may be of some assistance to readers who want to pursue these lines of thought.

1. Beginning Here

I first heard the story of the question of the Tsimshian chief while on a study tour of the Arctic in 2013. One of the other passengers on the Adventure Canada ship, a publisher of a magazine focused on the coastal arts of British Columbia, shared this story, which she had heard in a university lecture. I contacted her after the trip to ask her for the source. She made several efforts to do so, but was unable to run it to ground. Nevertheless, I believe it is a true story.

The concern that shapes these reflections is a desire to understand the significance of the Canadian context in all the dimensions of our lives: how we think about our lives, how we imagine our place in the world, our ways of organizing our lives economically, socially, politically, etc. I believe that this context also shapes and is shaped by the spiritual dimension of our lives. One could say that the reflections in this book could be called post-secular. They are open to the possibility that fundamental questions of our personal and political lives open beyond a one-dimensional view of life. The question of the Tsimshian chief opens up a fundamental concern of meaning that cannot and should not be limited to the one-dimensional materialism that has gripped both the communist and capitalist worlds. This post-secular view of politics was eloquently described by the Czech playwright and politician Vaclav Havel in his now famous Fourth of July address (Philadelphia, 1994), "The Need for Transcendence in the Postmodern World."

It is possible and imperative to think, at the same time, about the dispiriting dimensions of one's context and to articulate the realities that are particularly inspiring. The poet, farmer and thinker Wendell Berry has drawn out the ultimate dimensions of our economic context: "The question immediately and at least is economic: What is wrong with the way we are keeping house, the way we make our living, the way we live? (What is wrong with our minds?) And to take the economic question seriously enough is right away to ask another that is also but not only economic: What is happening to our souls?" (*A Small Porch,* p. 79).

However, these reflections are not what is usually called theological. They could more appropriately be called the "groundwork" for theology. These are considerations that take the context of Canada seriously, in a way that could be helpful for those who are seeking meaning and purpose in life, regardless of any specific religious commitments.

The concern for context has generated a wide variety of what are called "contextual theologies." The variety reflects different contextual realities: for example, liberation theologies in Latin America, the more communal (Ubuntu) realities of Africa; the Minjung or silent suffering of Korea; the anti-imperial theologies (feminist and black theologies) that have developed within the context of the United States.

The key thinkers on the variety of contextual theologies would be Douglas John Hall in his magisterial three-volume study *Thinking the Faith: Christian Theology in a North American Context*; and Robert Schreiter and Stephen B. Bevans of the Catholic Theological Union in Chicago, who have been pioneers in articulating the imperative of developing meaningful contextual theologies. (See *The*

New Catholicity: Theology Between the Global and the Local by Robert Schreiter and *Models of Contextual Theology* by Stephen B. Bevans.) All three of these thinkers are aware of the possibility that giving too much attention and significance to a context can result in a dispiriting relativism. However, they are equally convinced that all theology is contextual and that the claims of western European–based theology to be "universal" reflect the imperialistic bias of Western theology. The most serious challenge for contextual theology is how to incorporate a global perspective of unity that does not flatten out differences in the search for uniformity.

For some of my preliminary articles on this theme, see my "Where Deep Joy Meets the Deep Suffering of the World" (*New Theology Review*, Vol. 23, No. 2 [2010], pp. 35–44) and "Naming the Context of North America" (Ron Rolheiser, ed., *Secularity and the Gospel*, pp. 135–50).

2. Where Is Here?

The figure of an "abashed" person, an "abashed" country or culture, is found in Michael Ondaatje's description of "the one born in this country who knows nothing of the place … He was a watcher, a corrector … He searched out things, collected things. He was an abashed man, an inheritance from his father. Born in Abashed, Ontario" (*In the Skin of a Lion*).

My indebtedness to Northrop Frye and his student Margaret Atwood will be evident throughout these reflections. I realize that it is rather easy to dismiss some of their insights as dated, given the world of difference that exists between the insights they articulated in the 1960s and '70s, in the early days of what has been called CanLit. Most obviously, we are no longer so overwhelmed by the forces of nature that they describe so vividly and accurately. Nevertheless, the mindset and patterns of response in the face of overwhelming realities remains. The shape of Canadian culture has changed, but the dynamic remains the same. (See Linda Hutcheon, "Eruptions of Postmodernity: The Postcolonial and Ecological," in *Essays on Canadian Writing* Nos. 51–56 [Winter 93–Spring 94], 146–63.) Frye himself points this out in his 1963 Massey Lectures.

The key references for Northrop Frye remain *The Bush Garden: Essays on the Canadian Imagination* and *Divisions on a Ground: Essays on Canadian Culture.* The key reference for Margaret Atwood's insights into the dynamics of the imperative of survival and the various victim stances in a colonial context are found throughout her *Survival: A Thematic Guide to Canadian Literature.*

Frye recognizes the way in which the colonial context stunts the imagination. "The colonial position of Canada is therefore a frostbite at the roots of the Canadian imagination."

For an excellent description of the dilemma of "naming" a context that does not know its own words, see Dennis Lee, "Cadence, Country, Silence: Writing in Colonial Space," in *Canadian Poetry Online.*

Thomas King has named the narrative of Indigenous peoples in North America in his *The Inconvenient Indian: A Curious Account of Native People in North America.*

My reflections on the "location" of culture have been shaped by the writings of Wendell Berry: see his essay "Imagination and Place." My understanding of the dynamic/ existential reality of culture (as opposed to a more fixed/ essentialist view of someone like Samuel Huntington) has been influenced by the writings of Edward Said (*Culture and Imperialism*) and Homi Bhabha (*The Location of Culture*).

For a more extensive critique of the culturally induced dissatisfaction of consumerism, see my *Radical Gratitude.*

I refer there to the statistics used by John Kavanaugh in his *Following Christ in a Consumer Culture*: that is, the average American will, by the end of his or her life, have consumed three solid years of advertising alone. His book was written in 1991, so it is reasonable to assume that this is a modest estimate. See "How Much Media? 2013 Report on American Consumers" (produced by the Institute for Communication Technology Management at USC Marshall School of Business and James E. Short). That study suggests that the average American consumes 15.5 hours of media a day. Richard Sennett's book *The Corrosion of Character* describes the relationships between the growing conservativism in mobile middle-class families.

For an impressive reflection on the basis of the struggle between being a consumer or a citizen, see Naomi Klein's *No Logo: Taking Aim at the Brand Bullies.*

The prose poem by Anne Michaels was printed in the *Toronto Star* on February 22, 2017. She is an unusual writer who has combined history with an archeology of memory.

3. Original Moment

The significance of the founding moment in relation to the history of political entities is articulated in Hannah Arendt's seminal work of political theory, *On Revolution.*

Frye's description of the persistence of the garrison mentality even when the conditions that engendered it have changed: "In a society which changes rapidly, many things happen that frighten us or make us feel threatened. People try to huddle more closely together when they feel frightened or threatened, and in that situation their clichés turn hysterical" (1963 Massey Lectures).

Two recent books have given us a sense of the complex relationships between the early settlers and the Indigenous peoples. John Ralston Saul's research suggests that the early settlers learned the art of compromise and negotiation from the Indigenous peoples and that these skills were then used in negotiating the delicate balance between the French and the English at the time of Confederation (see his *A Fair Country: Telling Truths about Canada*). Constitutional expert Peter Russell has rewritten the political history of Canada to reflect the fact that there are three founding peoples (Indigenous, French and English) and not two (the French and English of the more official histories of Canada. See *Canada's Odyssey: A Country Based on Incomplete Conquests.*

In referring to our "national possessiveness," I have drawn on some of the insights in C.B. Macpherson's seminal work *The Political Theory of Possessive Individualism: Hobbes to Locke.*

The destruction of Indigenous culture to make room for business and the culture of the European settlers is vividly described in *Clearing the Plains: Disease, Politics of Starvation, and the Loss of Aboriginal Life* by James Daschuk. This destruction was the underlying narrative of the thousands of witnesses who appeared before the Truth and Reconciliation Commission of Canada. For a more personal, and thereby more painful, description, read Thomas King, "A Million Porcupines Crying in the Dark" (CBC Massey Lectures, *The Truth about Stories: A Native Narrative*, 2003, pp. 91–119).

Justice Thomas Berger's *Fragile Freedoms: Human Rights and Dissent in Canada* brings together the various historical examples of how those who seem strange and different have been excluded from the Canadian garrison. A wider consideration is available in Ian Radforth's "Ethnic Minorities and Wartime Injustices: Redress Campaigns and Historical Narratives in Late Twentieth-Century Canada," in *Settling and Unsettling Memories: Essays in Canadian Public History* (Nicole Neatby and Peter Hodgins, eds.).

For an excellent reference on the various dimensions of the North, see Sherrill E. Grace, *Canada and the Idea of North*, and Renée Hulan, *Northern Experience and the Myths of Canadian Culture*. In his 2011 CBC Massey Lectures, Adam Gopnick gives a multidimensional reflection on *Winter* as a defining experience in Canada.

For a vivid description of the toxic waste of Fort McMurray, see also *Tar Sands: Dirty Oil and the Future of a Continent*, by Andrew Nikiforuk, and the 2010 documentary film *Petropolis: Aerial Perspectives on the Alberta Tar Sands*, written and directed by Peter Mettler.

4. Spacious and Gracious

In grounding this reflection in the imagination of "the beginning," I am following a method set forth by Augustine in the fifth century, during the time of the decline of the Roman empire. He believed that an imaginative reflection on the beginnings of the world was the ground for the hope in its future. See Hannah Arendt's reflections on the significance of "the beginnings" in political theory of action in her doctoral thesis, *The Notion of Friendship in Augustine*.

For a wise and compelling articulation of an Indigenous perspective on creation, see *Braiding Sweetgrass: Indigenous Wisdom, Scientific Knowledge and the Teachings of Plants* by Robin Wall Kimmerer.

The centrality of the notion of Creation in a post-secular age has been most eloquently expressed in the essays and lectures by former Czech president and playwright Vaclav

Havel (see *The Art of the Impossible: Politics as Morality in Practice*). The phrase "a wrinkle in time" is taken from Madeleine L'Engle's book by the same title.

The Canadian poet Dennis Lee, in describing the significance of Canadian philosopher George Grant, noted that "reverence is more fully human than conquest or mastery." (See Lee's "Cadence, Country, Silence.")

The image of "dreams deferred" refers to Langston Hughes' poem "Harlem." The refrain "What we need is here" is a line from Wendell Berry's poem "The Wild Geese".

5. Grounds for Responsibility

Many of the insights in this chapter were set out in chapter 4 of my *Radical Gratitude*. There I outline the debilitating effects of an understanding of Power as control and the attendant sense of powerlessness that this creates. I suggest there that all too often, good people prefer a sense of powerlessness and victimhood because there is a moral innocence possible in such a stance. The fresh sense of power arises when power is reinterpreted as the energy to create which arises through interaction. This is laid out in the political theory of Hannah Arendt (in her *The Human Condition*) and in the writings of Michel Foucault on the "web" of power.

The exercise of power in the metropolis and the hinterland was first articulated by the Canadian economist Harold Innis in his classic study *The Fur Trade in Canada*. Although first articulated almost a century ago, this theory continues to generate relevant ideas for the economic reality of Canadian politics (see Mel Watkins, "Harold Innis: An Intellectual at the Edge of Empire," *Canadian Dimension*, July 7, 2006). His analysis of the economic history of Canada is also found in some major thinkers in the area of development studies.

The dynamic through which powerlessness is a self-fulfilling prophecy is brilliantly described by Michael Lerner in his *Surplus Powerlessness*.

The description of imperial power which is everywhere and nowhere is presented in *Empire* by Antonio Negri and Michael Hardt.

For a description of the spiritual crisis of the decline of the American empire, see the film by this name directed by Denis Arcand. See also Paul Kennedy's *The Rise and Fall of the Great Powers* and *Mortal Splendor: The American Empire in Transition* by Walter Russell Mead. A host of other books have appeared comparing the decline of Rome to the decline of America, such as *Are We Rome?* by Cullen Murphy and *America: The Farewell Tour* by Chris Hedges.

For a more detailed description of the collective power to survive that animated the first settler garrisons, see *Survival* by Margaret Atwood.

For a profound discussion of boundaries, otherness, identity and reconciliation, see Miroslav Volf, *Exclusion and Embrace: A Theological Exploration of Identity, Otherness, and Reconciliation*, written in the context of the conflicts of the former Yugoslavia.

6. What Are We For?

The contemporary discussion of the common good was instigated by an article published in 1968 by Garrett Hardin, "The Tragedy of the Commons." In this article he argued that resources that are owned in common will end up being overused. He used the example of a pasture held in common that was soon "over pastured" due to the lack of regulation of the resource. The article was not simply about overgrazing but also about population control and environmental regulation. Elinor Ostrom won the Nobel Prize in Economics in 2009 for challenging this view through her study of the capacity of local communities to regulate the use of common areas. See also Heather Menzies, *Reclaiming the Commons for the Common Good*, and Christopher Lind, *Rumours of a Moral Economy*.

The Natural City: Re-envisioning the Built Environment (Ingrid Leman Stefanovic and Stephen Bede Scharper, eds.) is a collection of creative new essays that try to reimagine the relationship between rural and urban environments.

For a passionate and clear-sighted reflection on the significance of climate change, see Naomi Klein's *This Changes Everything*. Maude Barlow and the Council of Canadians have been reminding us, forever it seems, of our responsibility for water. See her *Blue Future: Protecting Water for People and the Planet Forever*. For an astonishing view of the two million lakes in Canada, see *Lakeland: Journeys into the Soul of Canada* by Allan Casey.

Praise for *Why Are We Here?*

"Mary Jo Leddy, one of Canada's foremost and original spiritual explorers and a voice of those who arrive here as refugees, in this book offers a meditation on why we are together. It is a narrative of profound prose-poetry, a quest for the unifying and informing symbols of Canada. It will leave its readers in still, contemplative and grateful thought."

—**Michael Valpy,** journalist and a senior fellow of Massey College, University of Toronto

"Our Commission described Reconciliation as establishing and maintaining respectful relations between the First Peoples of the land and all Canadians, an uncomfortable disruption of the status quo. One of this country's deepest thinkers, revered human rights activist Mary Jo Leddy, draws upon decades of cross-cultural friendships and social justice engagement to offer spiritual introspection on this crucial juncture that is now *our* moment in history. *Why Are We Here? A Meditation on Canada* is a provocative meditation for our times."

—**Dr. Marie Wilson,** Commissioner, Truth and Reconciliation Commission of Canada, 2009–2015

"Prepare to be joyfully disrupted by Mary Jo's invitation to create communities of responsibility flowing from gratitude for the gift that is Canada. A beautiful offering of hope for our fractured relationships with Indigenous peoples and the earth at a time when most grapple with whether their efforts even begin to make a difference. Leddy leaves us certain we are powerfully weighing in with our lives and decisions, each day."

—**Sara Hildebrand,** founder and director of Millennium Kids

"Mary Jo Leddy is one of the most eloquent and important spiritual writers of our day. In this gracious meditation, we are awakened to a profound reflection on our proper role and place in a time of climate chaos, economic exclusion and perduring oppression of Indigenous lives and lifeways. Sifted through a lifetime of reflection, activism and deep hospitality, graced by stirring prose, this work leaves us both touched and tethered, invited to journey away from the dead zones of 'globalized indifference' and insatiable consumerism and into the vibrant waters of engaged solidarity."

—**Stephen Bede Scharper,** associate professor, School of the Environment, University of Toronto, and author of *For Earth's Sake: Toward a Compassionate Ecology* (Novalis); and **Hilary Cunningham Scharper,** a Canadian novelist and a professor of cultural anthropology at the University of Toronto

"Just as she describes refugee children as the 'eyes of her eyes and the ears of her ears,' Mary Jo Leddy provides us with a new lens through which to view the world around us. By asking the simple and profound question of 'Why are we here?' she challenges us to form new commitments to our communities and ourselves. In doing so she aims to make a country that is good and communities that will take responsibility for their own well-being."

—**Gavin Gardiner,** a Juno and Polaris prize–nominated songwriter and record producer who lives and works in the west end of Toronto

"Through the lens of her life and work, Mary Jo Leddy redefines the way so many of us see the people and the land that surround us. In asking, 'Why are we here?' she asks us to put aside the many boundaries that prevent us from answering the question honestly and with purpose. She challenges us to look outside of ourselves and to take responsibility for the communities we live in, and to recognize the fundamental role we each play in building them."

—**Sarah Creskey,** an artist who lives and works in the west end of Toronto

"Revealed in this profound meditation are provocative thoughts of who we are and how we need to be in order to be truly ourselves as Canadians. In her inimitable and thoughtful way, Mary Jo Leddy describes what it is 'to assume the particular blessing and burden of Canada.' I feel enriched by her revelations."

—**The Rt. Hon. Adrienne Clarkson,** 26th Governor General of Canada (1999–2005)

Thirty

Don called late in September. I was living in the kiddie-diddler's basement, his boiler room. It was the only place near Bernie I could afford. Maura and I still spoke, but we'd stopped going to the marriage counselor. Maura quit when the counselor suggested she take a break from having sex with Paul. There was talk of finding another counselor, one more amenable to Maura having sex with Paul, of inviting Paul to a session, even, but nothing happened. We were still, I believed, the loves of each other's life. But that life was maybe over now.

The kiddie-diddler was a kind and extremely unstable man named Harold. He had, as I suspected, once been in radio, voiced some very famous advertising campaigns. I no longer wondered why whenever he spoke I thought of a certain laundry detergent or strawberry-flavored milk.

Harold's brother Tommy slipped me extra cash to make sure Harold didn't wander the streets at night. Harold had dozens of stories he told over and over again, in the way of a man who has traveled the world, or never been anywhere at all. I listened to him talk less for the delight of his adventures than his timbre, his pitchman's pitch.

The shopping bag stuffed with shopping bags was never far from reach, but when I asked him its meaning or purpose he told me I didn't have the proper clearance. He let me look at his